Thankful Praise

THANKFUL PRAISE

A Resource for Christian Worship

Prepared for the use of the
Christian Church (Disciples of Christ)

by

Ronald J. Allen
Michael K. Kinnamon
Linda McKiernan-Allen
Katherine G. Newman Kinnamon
Keith Watkins

Edited by Keith Watkins

CBP Press
St. Louis, Missouri

Library of Congress Cataloging-in-Publication Data

Thankful praise.

1. Christian Church (Disciples of Christ)—Liturgy—Texts. 2. Christian Church (Disciples of Christ)—Liturgy. 3. Liturgies. 4. Public worship. I. Watkins, Keith. II. Allen, Ronald J. III. Christian Church (Disciples of Christ)
BX7325.T43   1987   264'.0663   86-24514
ISBN 0-8272-3650-6

Printed in the USA

CONTENTS

PREFACE

Thankful praise is the theme of the Christian life, shining through everything that Christians do and say. We experience life itself as a gift from God and the world around us as communion with the Holy One. Work and play, companionship with family and friends, even the tragedies of personal life and the terrors of history, are all tempered and redeemed by the surprising presence of the eternal Spirit.

Therefore, when Christians gather in Christ's name, every first day of the week, our strongest impulse is to express the joyful praise which wells up in our lives. With readings and songs, sermons and prayers, gifts and sacred meals, we exult in the life God gives, adore the One who loves so fully, give thanks for Jesus our savior and friend, and renew our promises to serve God faithfully.

Thankful Praise, the book, has one central purpose: to strengthen Christian public worship and especially the celebration of the Lord's Supper. It is addressed to one church family—the Christian Church (Disciples of Christ)—whose worship has always been built on the principle of "every Lord's Day the Lord's Supper." This book also has direct implications for other church bodies whose theologians are reclaiming the eucharistic center of the church's life and whose publishers are creating a new generation of liturgical books that foster worship at the Lord's Table.

The character of *Thankful Praise* is shaped by the fact that the celebration of the Lord's Supper among Disciples is distinctive. Local elders carry major responsibilities for every aspect of the service. The communion prayers, which ordinarily are offered by these elders, are usually brief, prepared specifically for each occasion, and they vary widely in content. Communion is very important to church members, but eucharistic piety and theology are given little attention in church teaching. The time has come for reclaiming the authentic Disciples tradition, for cutting away its limiting features, and for presenting a strong case for reform.

In this process, Disciples necessarily will be in dialogue with other churches and other movements for reformation. Although the several church traditions will continue their distinctive ways of life and worship, the destructive forms of division and isolation are being overcome. We can look forward to a time when the unity which Christ created as the foundation of the church will develop a historical form that all the world can recognize.

Two observations help to clarify the intentions of the authors. First, *Thankful Praise* contains prayers, calls to worship, and other resources that can be used as printed for Sunday worship. In that respect, it resembles other collections of liturgical materials currently available in English. *Thankful Praise* also contains extensive commentary with recommendations for practice that are designed to help readers understand the principles behind these printed resources. Our intention is not to provide an exhaustive compilation but to stimulate reflection about worship and to provide models for the local development of responsible and forceful worship materials. The book is, therefore, intended for pastors, elders, and others with responsibility for the preparation and leadership of the weekly service.

The second observation is that we do not intend to prescribe how all worship should take place in Disciples of Christ congregations, but neither do we intend simply to reinforce current Disciples practice. We take a strong stand about Disciples worship and its relationship to the universal church, with the result that some of our recommendations may seem foreign to many Disciples. We know of no better way to provoke dialogue and renewal than to present our position as persuasively as possible, even as we stress that ours is not the final word on worship in our tradition.

In shaping this volume, we have been guided by five principles:

—We seek to connect Disciples worship more firmly with the great tradition of Christian worship stemming from the time of the apostles and from the church of the first centuries after the resurrection of Christ.

—We seek to be responsive to the search for Christian unity in our era and to the agreements on liturgy growing out of such examples of theological convergence as the World Council of Churches' *Baptism, Eucharist and Ministry* and the Consultation on Church Union's *COCU Consensus*.

—We seek to be faithful to the crucial features of traditional

Disciples worship, including the important role of lay leadership, prayer that is created for each new celebration (as opposed to either standardized liturgies or purely spontaneous prayer), and to the preeminent place of the Lord's Supper.

—We seek to be sensitive to essential lessons from contemporary life, including the growing awareness of social injustice around the world and of the church's responsibility for addressing it, the post-Holocaust realization that Christian theology and worship have historically embodied anti-Jewish teachings with murderous consequences, and the fact that many persons have felt excluded by the traditional, frequently sexist, language of worship.

—We seek to enhance the beauty and diversity of worship in the Disciples of Christ by striving for language that is vivid, biblical, and felicitous; and by encouraging variety in the ordering of the service.

Behind our work is a deep concern for our church. Although the Disciples tradition has sources of strength and resilience, our contemporary life, and especially our worship, is frequently weak and lethargic.

We are convinced that the Disciples of Christ churches are poised for a period of creative growth and that the renewal of worship is the key.

This volume is offered as one contribution to that process. In our work we have remembered with gratitude two Disciples in the middle part of this century who enriched our church's understanding and practice of the Lord's Supper. In Britain, William Robinson influenced a generation of Disciples with his teaching and writings, including *The Administration of the Lord's Supper* (Birmingham: The Berean Press, 1947). In North America, G. Edwin Osborn shaped Disciples worship by his teaching and through the book which he edited, *Christian Worship: A Service Book* (St. Louis: The Bethany Press, 1953).

Thankful Praise is the result of a process that began in 1983 in conversations between Keith Watkins, professor of worship at Christian Theological Seminary, Peter Morgan, who carries the portfolio for worship for the Division of Homeland Ministries, and Herbert H. Lambert, editor of CBP Press. Watkins proposed that a small group of writers in Indianapolis, working independently and without financial subsidy, develop a book of services and prayers that could, with appropriate review, be offered to the Christian Church (Disciples of Christ) for study and trial use. A team of five writers and three consultants was formed.

During the three years of this project's life, the team met

frequently for brief periods of time and twice for three-day writers' conferences. The cost of these longer meetings was partially compensated by the Division of Homeland Ministries. Most of the costs of manuscript preparation have been paid from a faculty manuscript fund at Christian Theological Seminary. Publication costs at CBP Press have been partially offset by a grant from the Division of Homeland Ministries.

Throughout the development of this book, portions of the work were sent to reviewers. Pastors, elders, and other scholars with interest in worship were included in the list of people who were invited to comment on the team's work. All of these responses were studied; they have helped the team conceptualize this book and create the materials that it contains.

This book is similar in purpose to volumes that have been published by other churches (including Episcopal, Lutheran, United Methodist, Presbyterian, and United Church of Christ) in the process of developing new service books. These churches have published preliminary studies that contain theological essays and proposals for the reform of worship. After some years of study, use, and evaluation, these preliminary books are revised and their contents contribute to the new book that is finally published.

The consultants and writers and their positions at the time of publication, are listed below:

Consultants

William H. Edwards, Director of Special Congregational Resources; Louise B. Evans, Director of Family and Children's Ministries; and Peter M. Morgan, Director of Membership and Worship, from the staff of the Division of Homeland Ministries of the Christian Church (Disciples of Christ).

Writers

Ronald J. Allen, Assistant Professor of Preaching and New Testament; Michael K. Kinnamon, Assistant Professor of Theology; Keith Watkins, Professor of Worship and Director for Advanced Professional Studies (all from the faculty of Christian Theological Seminary, Indianapolis); Katherine G. Newman Kinnamon, Associate Regional Minister of the Christian Church in Indiana; Linda McKiernan-Allen, *ad interim* Associate Minister, First Christian Church, Noblesville, Indiana. Much of the manuscript preparation was done by Margaret Darnell, Karen Kelm, and Joy Sherrill.

The faculty members of the team have been encouraged in this project, both personally and institutionally, by Richard Dickinson, then dean, and T. J. Liggett, then president, of Christian Theological Seminary. The writers are pleased that this book is being published during Dr. Liggett's term as moderator of the Christian Church (Disciples of Christ); and they hereby express gratitude for his long ministry as pastor, missionary, mission executive, theological educator, and leader in the life of the church and the world.

A Note About Copyright

Most materials in this book have been developed by the writers, as new compositions or as extensively edited resources, in most cases not previously published. Many of the compositions and other resources use phrases or ideas drawn from Scripture, usually the Revised Standard Version. Even when resources follow the scripture text quite closely, the passages have usually been adapted freely for liturgical use.

The writers intend this book to be useful both as a volume from which worship leaders read and as the source for materials that are reproduced in church bulletins for the congregation. The copyright notice at the beginning of the book indicates the boundaries of authorized reproduction of the contents of the volume. Liturgical materials are numbered in a continuous series throughout this volume.

Within the limits indicated above, these materials may be reproduced for liturgical and educational uses in churches and schools without asking written permission of the publisher. Any reproduction offered for sale, however, requires special permission in writing. Some of the contents of this book are copyrighted by other publishers. These publishers have given permission for the reprinting of these materials in *Thankful Praise*. All of these items may be read from this book in public worship or at other times. The holders of the copyright, however, may have imposed restrictions on reproduction. The writers, consultants, and CBP Press expect the users of *Thankful Praise* to observe ethical and legal principles in regard to the use of copyrighted materials.

The Season After Pentecost, 1986

THE RENEWAL OF WORSHIP

All across the world there is a significant move to rediscover authentic Christian worship. People in our congregations want to be intimately related to God, even though religious experience often seems so remote to daily life. Like the Samaritan woman to whom Jesus spoke, we yearn for living water that will quench the dryness of our spirits. Like the people of Galilee, we crave food that will satisfy the hunger for meaning in life, a hunger that never seems to go away. We come to church, Sunday after Sunday, to respond to God's gracious love. As we sing, pray, preach, and commune at the Lord's table, we hope that this renewing encounter with God will take place, that the dryness of our spirits will be refreshed, that the weakness of our moral resolves will be made strong again.

What we often meet, however, is something far less than what we yearn for: hollow words, confusing ideas, sluggish ceremonies, all fragile as pressed flowers in the family Bible. Even when our services are deliberately made contemporary, they often lose their ability to satisfy and sustain, leaving us with the remembrance of energy and excitement but without the power to support our efforts to love God and one another. The rediscovery of authentic Christian worship—this is surely one of the greatest needs in churches today.

THE FOUNDATION OF CHRISTIAN WORSHIP

Worship is our response to God, to the One who is our rock and our salvation. In one sense, therefore, all of life should be worship. The term is generally used, however, in a more restricted sense to mean the gathering of a community of believers for a corporate expression of thankful praise.

Christian worship has its roots in the life of ancient Israel—its Temple prayers and sacrifices, its family celebrations (especially the Sabbath meal and Passover Seder), and its tradition of scriptural study and prayer in the synagogue. These practices were adapted by Jesus, reshaped by the church of the first century as it met to praise God through the memorial of Christ's life, death, and resurrection, and handed down, in a rich variety of forms, by subsequent generations of Christians. At every point in this long history, Christian worship is colored through and through with the grandeur and glory of God. Although the prayers, hymns, and ceremonies have changed through the centuries, their common spirit is captured in the ancient verse:

Holy, holy, holy Lord, God of power and might:
Heaven and earth are full of your glory.
Hosanna in the highest.

For Christians this thankful praise to God has made use of two activities that are universal in the human family: *coming together* and *sharing food*. These activities are so constant a part of life that we can do them without thinking, without needing to remind ourselves of their primary purposes. For this very reason, they can become the occasion for accomplishing other life functions. Assemblies and meal times become parties and banquets, convocations and testimonial dinners, political rallies and religious rituals. Something deeply rooted in our common human experience is thus the carrier of uncommon meanings about life and death, and about God and the universe.

Coming together is at the center of our life with Jesus, for he said that where two or three are gathered together in his name he is in their midst (Matthew 18:20). In their assemblies, Christians sing songs of praise, tell stories of the faith, offer prayers, and contribute to the needs of others. Since apostolic times, Christians have also met around a table to share a special feast of bread and wine. The early Christians called this form of worship *eucharistia*, which in Greek means thanksgiving. This religious act, which often is called the Lord's Supper, Holy Communion, or Eucharist, has been for millions of believers a uniquely effective means of realizing communion with Christ and each other, for making Christ's sacrifice a real part of their lives, and for anticipating the time of God's reign throughout creation.

ONE FAMILY, MANY BRANCHES

The eucharistic service, including both proclamation of the Word and sharing of the sacred meal, was the unquestioned form of Christian worship for 1500 years. During the Protestant Reformation, however, new theological convictions, and new forces in the wider society, brought about significant changes in the ways that Christians worshiped. For the majority of Protestants today, the normal Sunday service does not include communion. Furthermore, the ways that the several churches celebrate the eucharist now vary widely.

Some church traditions use prayers that are written in their worship books, express a highly developed theology of the Lord's Supper, convey a deep sense of mystery, and are repeated week after week with only slight variation throughout the year. In these churches—Orthodox, Roman Catholic, Lutheran, and Anglican—the theology of the Lord's Supper stresses the action of God in this meal and the powerful connection of the meal and its participants with Jesus. Services in these churches are marked by reverence and awe. There is a strong sense that people come together because God expects them to do it and because their own eternal destiny is at stake in the way they conduct their assemblies and religious feasts (Hebrews 12:28-29).

At the other extreme of Christian practice are church families that emphasize the exuberant gathering of their members, with little interest in the ancient festival of the eucharistic meal. If any one trait characterizes this broad band of Christian practice, it is the desire that life be open to new outpourings of the Holy Spirit. These Christians find their model in events like the Day of Pentecost when established routines were overpowered by dramatic movements of the Spirit. Worshipers are to be free to speak as the Spirit gives them words to say (see Acts 2:4 and 1 Corinthians 12—14).

Even in these churches public worship gradually assumes patterns of speech and ceremony that repeat themselves week after week. Yet there is a readiness to let the patterns be altered by the experiences and concerns of the moment. In their words and actions, Christians in these churches strive for directness and unpretentiousness, and there often is a strong sense of religious excitement. Something happens that goes beyond normal human experience, something described as the visitation of the Holy Spirit. Preaching, praying, and praising are the major elements of worship in this part of the Christian family, with the eucharistic meal an infrequent and relatively unimportant part of their worshiping life.

Standing between these two groups of churches is a third portion of the Christian family, a broad spectrum that includes Methodists, Presbyterians, the United Church of Christ, some Baptist churches, and the Disciples. In theory these churches give equal importance to coming together around the word of God and sharing in the Lord's Supper. In the regular practice of these churches, except for the Disciples, the service of praise, preaching, and prayer is the major partner, with the service at the Lord's table usually taking place monthly or quarterly. In all of their services, the churches of this third group strive for balance between order and spontaneity, prescribed texts and extemporaneous prayers, stylized ceremonial and direct, natural movements. They want worship to be serious, but not solemn, reverent but not mysterious, warm and open but not boisterous (see 1 Corinthians 14; Hebrews 12:25-29).

CHRISTIAN CHURCH (DISCIPLES OF CHRIST)

While it is true that Disciples belong more with the middle group than the other two, we are a difficult church to categorize. Our founders came from Presbyterian backgrounds. Many of their ideas were drawn from the evangelical movements of the nineteenth century, but they undertook their own careful examinations of scripture to search for the authentic forms of church practice. This combination of heartfelt religion and biblically authenticated structures gave them their distinctive approach to worship.

These Disciples agreed with other Protestants in their preference for expository preaching, extemporaneous praying, and evangelical singing. What set them apart was their insistence upon the weekly "breaking of the loaf in commemoration of Christ's death." The celebration of the Lord's Supper, they contended, was the reason for coming together on the Lord's Day. They believed, furthermore, in a form of pastoral leadership that was rooted in the life of the congregation and community. The people of a congregation would select two or three persons from their own membership to be their leaders. These "elders" were charged to oversee the congregation's religious life and to take the lead in Sunday worship. Although they were neither seminary trained nor salaried, they were ordained to the office of bishop or elder and presided over communion week after week. Thus, worship could always be eucharistic; there was no need to wait for professional clergy. Since these congregations did not use prayer books, the content and quality of their leadership in worship varied widely.

This interest in eucharistic worship was more devotional than theological, more focused upon the experience of communion with God and one another than upon explanations of how this communion takes place. Even today, when our church people are asked to talk about communion, a common description of what the service means is that this is the time during worship when we feel closest to God.

From our beginnings, we Disciples have trusted congregations to organize the parts of the service according to their own criteria, though we have agreed that the two main components of worship are preaching and communion. The major difference among congregations has been the relation of sermon and supper—which comes early in the service and which comes late? The early practice seems to have been the placing of the communion at the final, climactic point of the service. Around the beginning of the twentieth century, it became common practice for the sermon to come at that place of highest significance. The trend since the 1950s has been to return to the earlier pattern with communion coming as a response to and fulfillment of the proclamation of God's Word.

By emphasizing the Lord's Supper as the primary act of worship, Disciples are similar to several other major church families, especially Orthodox, Roman Catholic, Lutheran, and Episcopalian. Yet in the style, pattern, and tone of worship, we have generally taken our lead from the Methodist, United Church of Christ, and Presbyterian churches. These traditions have built their worship around preaching, praise, and prayer rather than communion.

Disciples worship, at its best, has drawn effectively on both parts of this heritage. Yet worship in many Disciples congregations is today less vigorous than it ought to be. Our celebrations of the Lord's Supper often seem to have lost their connection to the historic faith that gives them depth and seem out of touch with contemporary sources of spiritual energy. Thus, in Disciples congregations, too, the life of thankful praise is in great need of renewal.

PRINCIPLES OF RENEWAL

During recent years many churches have experimented, separately and together, in the effort to be faithful to their own life and to find renewal. It is now possible to identify six convictions or principles which are emerging from this period of liturgical reform, principles which may help Disciples as we, too, think afresh about the purpose, pattern, and practice of Christian worship.

1. *Authentic worship is rooted in the church's experience of the gospel, especially as it is expressed in the Bible and in the church's living experience through history.* Churches are rediscovering the significance of "recital," the importance of retelling in worship the wonderful deeds of God. From the Exodus and Easter to contemporary examples of new birth, from Abraham to Mother Teresa and Desmond Tutu, these stories show how our own lives may be shaped by God. The touchstone for comprehending God's action in our lives is most certainly scripture; but scripture itself is a product of the early Christian community and is necessarily reinterpreted in each succeeding generation if it is to be a living witness to the love and power of God.

Scripture and "tradition" thus form an inseparable basis for our worship (something Disciples have not always appreciated). Together they testify that the disclosure of God-in-Christ to which the Bible witnesses is a living, present reality. To say that worship is rooted in scripture, therefore, is not simply a call for solemn recollection of what God once did, but an acknowledgment that worship is encounter with the divine here and now.

2. *Worship is deeply and inevitably theological.* Worship expresses ideas about God, God's relationship to the world, and the world's response to God. Other aspects of theology are also implied in worship, including ideas about Jesus Christ and the Holy Spirit, the church, salvation, and the meaning of life. This theological quality is present in the service as a whole; but also in its parts from the order of its parts to the wording of all that is spoken or sung, to the manner in which the service is conducted. Thus the key question for the service as a whole and all its parts is this: Does this act of worship speak the truth? Decisions about worship are sometimes made on the basis of practicality: "Will it work?" This criterion, though useful, is incomplete. Prior to every other criterion for worship is that of faithfulness to the will of God.

3. *The church encompasses significant diversity in the theological positions*

on which its worship is based. Principles two and three must be held together, for the church contains not *one* but *several* theologies, all of which are intended to witness to the one true and living God.

Is worship primarily a matter of God's gift (grace) or of our human response to that gift (faith)? Most churches are now able to answer "both." Christ's presence at the Lord's Supper, for example, does not depend upon our faith, for that would limit the freedom of God; but we now agree that faith is needed to discern the presence of our Lord. Communion is indeed a gift of God, but it is also the worshipful celebration of a believing community.

To take another example, is worship primarily a remembrance of God's saving acts or an anticipation of God's sovereign reign which is to come? Do we emphasize the great tradition of Christian witness or the dynamic presence of the Spirit which opens us to the possibility of genuine newness? Again, the churches in ecumenical discussion are able to resist either/or answers, insisting that authentic anticipation is rooted in the memory of what God has done for our salvation.

Disciples have long espoused a commitment to theological diversity. What this has often meant, however, is simply a lack of attention to theological issues, leaving the patterns of our worship to be determined by functional considerations. An authentic appreciation of diversity should lead us to take theology more seriously, not less so. While we happily acknowledge that there is no one correct way to offer thankful praise, it remains true that "as we worship, so shall we believe." Every tradition thus needs to give close attention to the theology expressed in its worship.

4. *Worship is intimately connected with the church's mission, including its struggles for peace and justice in the world.* This connection goes back to Christianity's Jewish heritage in which sacrifice, meditation on the law, and a life of obedience to God are intertwined. Christians, however, have often forgotten, or preferred to ignore, this relationship between worship and mission. Worship, they argue, is something that happens between individuals and God at certain specified times and places and should not be confused with social concerns.

The churches involved in the new consensus on worship have strongly rejected this line of thinking. The experience of God's presence in worship should lead, they argue, to responsible care for God's creation, and especially for those creatures who bear God's image. Thankful praise is rendered not just by what we say and think but by what we do. God is glorified through the lives of

Christians in the world, even as those lives are renewed and sustained by coming together and sharing food in worship.

The very language of worship can reflect a commitment to justice. Many Christians now believe that their worship will be renewed only when its language moves beyond the traditional masculine bias with its unjust exclusion of women. This book affirms this belief and strives for language that is inclusive of both genders, and thereby reflective of the whole people of God.

5. *While worship involves ideas that are timeless and universal, it should be expressed through the culture of the local worshiping community.* This principle may seem obvious, but it masks difficulties and dangers. On the one hand, the unity of the church demands that Christian worship in each place be recognizable as such to Christians from other contexts. We share the same Lord, the same faith, the same baptism, the same scripture across all differences of language and culture. Surely our worship should reflect this universal inheritance.

On the other hand, people must hear the gospel and pray to God in speech that is their own, using art and ritual borrowed from their distinctive contexts. The modern consensus regarding worship recognizes that such contextualization inevitably takes place. The task is to encourage this process, while at the same time, insisting that the indigenous elements be carriers of the Gospel that transcends all particular ideas and experiences.

6. *Worship should be both open to creative transformation and conformed to enduring standards in its meaning and patterns.* The churches have been divided into two groups: those that require the use of officially prescribed books and services and those that expect ministers and congregations to order worship locally. Today, the two groups are moving much closer together. Although they still use officially required service books, Catholics, Lutherans, and Episcopalians have increased the choices that may be made by leaders of worship, and the mood of these prayers and services is very much like the mood that has characterized free church worship. The new publications of churches in the Methodist and Presbyterian families are examples of movement in the other direction. While continuing to value freedom of choice in the congregations, these churches are giving much more attention than before to sacramental worship and to form and order in their services.

A RESOURCE FOR RENEWAL

The principles described above have deeply influenced this

resource. Though focused on worship in the Christian Church (Disciples of Christ), this book attempts to be consistent with the agreements that are emerging in ecumenical discussion concerning the shape, language, and meaning of Christian worship.

"Shape" refers to the structure or outline of the service, the skeleton that supports the words and coordinates the actions. Here early Disciples practice and the ecumenical convergence agree that worship features the proclamation of the Word of God, *followed* by the enacting and embodying of that Word in Holy Communion, all in a setting rich with hymnody and prayer. This shape is presupposed throughout *Thankful Praise* and is elaborated in the following commentary.

The "language" of worship is important both as a means to communicate ideas and as an expression of the spirit of the service. When the language is too formal, technical, or archaic, it inhibits communication and suggests relationship to God that is distant. Yet language of the other extreme—informal, colloquial, or pop— gives the impression that worship is trivial and that any ideas are satisfactory as long as they are enthusiastic and sincere. The editors of this book have concentrated on using serious biblical speech that talks about divine mysteries in ways that everyone can understand. As in other newly-published worship books and Bible translations, God is praised in language that is at home in our time.

"Meaning" refers to the ideas that services express. The following materials defy easy summary, but in general they affirm that worship is essentially corporate thanksgiving and praise offered by sinful and redeemed human beings in response to God's saving revelation. Since Christians look to Jesus Christ as God's decisive self-disclosure, Christian worship is the church's celebration and memorial of God's reconciling love given in Christ as well as its prayerful anticipation of the day when Christ's reign shall be complete. We affirm that such worship is made possible through the Holy Spirit whose power we invoke and gratefully acknowledge.

Although the service as a whole expresses this theological meaning, the most concise statement of it is in the communion prayers. Thus, *Thankful Praise* gives extensive attention to this portion of the worship service. What we say to God at the communion table is more significant than any other set of words in the service.

Careful reflection on the Lord's Supper is particularly important for Disciples, given our practice of using elders at the Table, to offer communion prayers, and help to distribute the elements. This book, in line with recent ecumenical discussion, and for reasons outlined later, urges that an ordained minister "preside" at the Lord's Table by saying the words of institution; but it also seeks to preserve the role of the elders by exploring new patterns for praying over the loaf and the cup. This book also enlarges the role of the congregation in communion.

The mystery of our salvation is so rich and complex that no one Sunday service can express it all. Over the course of the year, however, it is possible to move across the range of this mystery, from birth to resurrection, from the covenant with Abraham to the eschatological banquet. That is why the recovery of the Liturgical Year as an organizing principle for Christian worship is one of the most promising trends for the renewal of our worship life. The materials for worship in *Thankful Praise* are arranged according to this pattern of Advent, Christmas, Epiphany, Lent, Easter, and Pentecost.

Finally, God as Holy Spirit is the cause of renewal. This Spirit is like the wind, blowing where it wills. None of our efforts alone can bring life to the church. Yet this same Spirit calls us to be open and receptive and to work. Therefore, the encouragement which Paul offered to the Corinthian church is also appropriate for churches today: "Be steadfast, immovable, always abounding in the work of the Lord, knowing that in the Lord your labor is not in vain" (1 Corinthians 15:58).

A NOTE ABOUT THE TITLE DEACON

In *Thankful Praise* all terms for leaders of worship include both women and men. Pastor, minister, elder, worship leader, and choir director make no distinctions in gender.

We also use the word *deacon* as an office that includes women as well as men, thus reclaiming for Disciples the way that this word is used in Scripture. In the epistles, deacon (Greek *diakonos*) refers both to women and men (see Philippians 1:1; Romans 16:1; 1 Timothy 3:8,12). Romans 16:1 may be confusing because Phoebe is identified in English translations as a "deaconess." The Greek word, however, is *diakonos* which in all other occurrences in the apostolic writings is translated "deacon." Furthermore, because Greek uses the same word for "wife" and "woman" (*gune*), it can be concluded that 1 Timothy 3:11 refers not to the wives of male deacons but to women who are serving in the same capacity.

The use of deacon to include men and women also overcomes clumsy usage that has developed among Disciples since the mid-1970s. In order to overcome the gender distinctive use of deaconess and deacon, Disciples began to use the collective noun diaconate. Prior to that time men and women generally performed different service functions. Women, called deaconesses, performed the largely invisible roles of preparing the elements and cleaning up afterwards. Men, called deacons, served the elements to the people in public worship. It now is common practice for these two acts of ministry to be combined. Women prepare, serve, and clean up. Men prepare, serve, and clean up. They should bear the same title.

Furthermore, the word diaconate is awkward to use. One cannot accurately say, "She is a diaconate" any more than one could say, "She is an eldership." One has to say that he or she is a "member of the diaconate." The use of the collective noun gives an impersonal sound. "The diaconate will serve" is more mechanical than "the elders will serve."

This book uses the word deacon without gender distinction. It assumes that scripture is correct to use this strong word for women who serve and for men who serve.

AN ORDER FOR
THE SUNDAY SERVICE

(pages 24-27)

AN ORDER FOR
THE SUNDAY SERVICE

THE COMMUNITY COMES TOGETHER
TO SERVE GOD IN WORSHIP[a]

Gathering of the Community[b]
Opening Music
Greeting
Hymn[c]
Opening Prayer(s)

THE COMMUNITY PROCLAIMS
THE WORD OF GOD

First Reading from the Bible[d]
Psalm or Other Response[e]
Second Reading from the Bible
Anthem or Other Response
Reading from the Gospel
Sermon

THE COMMUNITY RESPONDS TO
THE WORD OF GOD

Call to Discipleship
Hymn
Affirmation of Faith
Prayers of the People
24

[a] The headings to the five sections of the service deliberately emphasize the corporate character of worship. It is possible, however, to shorten them as follows: Coming Together to Serve God in Worship, Proclaiming the Word of God, Responding to the Word, Coming Together Around the Lord's Table, Going Forth in Mission.

[b] Elements considered essential to the Sunday service are indicated in **bold type**. While the basic pattern of this service is strongly recommended, the details are flexible. The first hymn, for example, could easily precede the greeting or follow the opening prayer.

[c] Music, especially communal singing, is vital to Christian worship. There is no particular point, however, at which the singing of hymns is essential. The hymn usually included in the time of "coming together" is normally a hymn of praise. Other hymns (this order suggests three) should reflect the distinctive character of the moments in the service when they occur.

[d] The reading from the Bible is essential to Christian worship. While three scriptural readings are recommended in the following commentary, this number is not an absolute requirement. The first reading is ordinarily from the Hebrew Scriptures, and the third reading ordinarily comes from one of the four Gospels. The second reading comes from another part of the Apostolic Writings.

[e] A children's sermon, if used, may come at this point in the service.

THE COMMUNITY COMES TOGETHER
AROUND THE LORD'S TABLE

Invitation to the Lord's Table
Offering[f]
Prayers at the Table[g]
Words of Institution and Breaking of the Bread
Lord's Prayer[h]
Peace[i]
Communion
Prayer After Communion

THE COMMUNITY GOES FORTH
TO SERVE GOD IN MISSION

Hymn
Closing Words[j]
Closing Music

[f] The offering is part of the service in which the congregation brings gifts of money and the communion elements, and with these sets the table. A musical response, prayer of dedication, and communion hymn may be included.

[g] The following commentary includes several models for prayer at the table. Each includes the major themes of this climactic act of worship: thankful praise, remembrance of Jesus, prayer for the Holy Spirit, and renewal of the covenant with God. The words of institution are always included as warrant, as part of the prayers, or as the words said when the bread is broken.

[h] The Lord's Prayer concludes the prayers at the table. It may come earlier in the service, perhaps as part of the "prayers" preceding the "offering."

[i] The peace also may come at other points in the service—for example, following a prayer of confession before the readings from scripture.

[j] The closing words often precede the final hymn.

COMMENTARY ON THE ORDER FOR THE SUNDAY SERVICE

THE COMMUNITY COMES TOGETHER TO SERVE GOD IN WORSHIP

Gathering of the Community

The congregation will be prepared for worship if three things happen as the time for the service draws near. First, the congregation symbolically re-establishes its identity as community. Second, the congregation is oriented to the service itself. Third, a boundary is drawn between the many times and places in which we encounter God and one another during the week and this one time and place in which, through liturgical words and acts, our whole lives are brought into focus and invested with the meaning of the Gospel.

When the congregation comes to offer service to God through worship, members often have been separated from one another by seven days or longer, and they bring widely varied experiences. The members of the congregation need to renew their relationships and to re-establish their sense of community. Thus, members greet one another informally in the narthex or sanctuary with a word, a touch. Pastors may find that a good way to prepare for worship is to mingle with the people as they are gathering.

This period of gathering can be a time for a leader of the congregation to welcome the worshipers, to interpret the season of the Christian year, to announce a theme for that Sunday, to point out aspects of the service which require extra attention for full congregational participation, to introduce the leaders of worship, and to practice hymns or liturgical acts which will be used later in the service.

Three kinds of announcements are appropriate during worship: (1) orientation to the service (as described above), (2) pastoral information of concern to the whole community (e.g., births, marriages, illnesses, deaths), and (3) events in the life of the congregation (e.g., meetings, dinners, special celebrations or projects). Placement of these announcements can certainly vary from place to place and from time to time. Some may wish to put them at different points in the order of worship: orientation to the service during the period of gathering, pastoral information preceding the prayers of the people (pastoral prayer), congregational events toward the end of worship as a way of anticipating the going forth. Others may wish to make all announcements during the time of gathering or at the close of the service.

Opening Music

The symbolic boundary between normal time and the sacred time of worship is often drawn musically. The familiar term "prelude" is not used in this order of service because it implies something that happens before the main event. The opening music, however, is an integral part of worship, inviting the congregation to empty itself of prideful preoccupations and to enter fully into this special period of thankful praise to the One who alone deserves it.

The opening music is brief and, while usually performed in North American churches on an organ, need not be so limited. Dance, mime or other visual activities may also be appropriate on occasion. Whatever the form, the opening music (or activity) should reflect the character of that particular service. Thus, during Lent, the music would be quite meditative; during Easter, celebrative.

Many congregations have attendants, sometimes called acolytes, bring light into the sanctuary (usually by lighting candles on the communion table) during the opening music. In this way the congregation is reminded of the God who lights our darkness and around whom the community gathers.

Greeting

In the greeting the congregation acknowledges the presence of God in a way similar to the salutation of friends in joyous reunion. The greeting may declare the worth of God, acknowledge our readiness to hear God speak, express the confidence that God will touch us in a significant way in the time of worship, affirm our openness to one another as channels of God's presence and grace, or offer our lives to God's use during the service of worship.

The greeting has traditionally been cast in one of two forms: the Call to Worship or the Ascription of Praise. These are alternative forms which, while usually spoken, can also be sung or dramatized.

The *Call to Worship*, as the title suggests, is addressed to the congregation (not to God) and is, therefore, not a prayer. The Call states why the community has gathered by stressing the general themes of worship: praise and thanksgiving to the Author of our creation and redemption. Frequently the Call to Worship will be taken from a passage of scripture such as I Chronicles 16:23-25:

1   Sing to the Lord, all the earth!
Tell of God's salvation from day to day.
Declare God's glory among the nations,
God's marvelous works among all the peoples!
For great is the Lord, and greatly to be praised.

The format of the Call to Worship may vary. It can be voiced by the worship leader alone, said in unison, or read responsively by leader and congregation. The following example illustrates the joining of biblical and contemporary imagery in an antiphonal (alternating) format:

2   A.   Come, let us celebrate the supper of the Lord.
B.   Let us make a huge loaf of bread
and let us bring abundant wine
as at the wedding feast of Cana.
A.   Let the women not forget the salt,
B.   let the men bring the yeast.
All.   Let the guests come,
the lame, the blind, the crippled, the poor.
A.   Come quickly.
Let us follow the recipe of the Lord.
B.   All of us, let us knead the dough together
with our hands.
All.   Let us see with joy
how the bread grows.

A.   Because today we celebrate the meeting
         with the Lord.
B.   Today we renew our commitment to God.[1]

An *Ascription of Praise* is directed to God by, or in the presence of, the congregation and is usually drawn from scripture.

3   I will bless you, God!
     You fill the world with awe:
     You dress yourself in light,
     rich, majestic light.
     You pitched the sky like a tent,
     built your house beyond the rain.
     You ride upon the clouds,
     the wind your wings,
     the wind your words,
     the fire your willing tongues.
                    (Psalm 104:1-4)[2]

The content of the greeting may change with the liturgical season (Advent greetings being more anticipatory, Lenten greetings reflecting a more penitential mood), but the purpose of this part of the service remains constant: to acknowledge and express that our worship is a God-centered activity. A strong, positive greeting is, thus, an important foundation for all that follows.

Hymn
     The importance of singing in the life of Israel and the church is indicated by Moses: "The Lord is my strength and my song . . ." (Exodus 15:2). The musical tradition is long and varied: the song of Miriam (Exodus 15:21), one of the oldest fragments of the Bible; the Psalms; the hymns of the early church (e.g., 1 Timothy 3:16); medieval chant; musical settings of Reformation theology; traditional spirituals; gospel songs; and works of contemporary composers. Through all of these the people of God have expressed their faith in song.
     Often the first hymn is a joyous, elevating song of praise, thus lifting again the central theme of Christian worship. There are times, however, when other themes and moods may be more appropriate. During Lent, for example, a more contemplative

---

[1]Numbered notations refer to editorial comments and are printed at the end of this chapter, beginning on p. 56.

opening hymn may better orient the congregation to the character of the season.

In some services worship leaders, including the choir, walk without ceremony to their seats during the opening music. In others, however, a more formal procession of leaders and choir takes place during the initial hymn. The former suggests that the true choir of worship is the congregation itself. The latter emphasizes the solemnity of worship and dramatizes our entry into sacred space. The point is not that one is right and the other wrong, but that choices made about worship, even those of movement and gesture, usually carry theological implications and, therefore, deserve careful consideration.

Opening Prayer(s)

In one sense prayer refers to all aspects of humanity's conscious relationship to God. Thus, Paul exhorts the Thessalonians to "pray constantly" (1 Thess. 5:17-18). The term is also used, however, to describe purposeful acts of communication with God, and, even more specifically, to denote those words which we—individually or communally, silently or orally—address to God. God, the eternal Spirit, acts in prayer (though in ways we often cannot fathom), and through prayer the community opens itself to the powerful, active presence of God.

Prayer, therefore, is central to Christian worship, coming at several points in the service. The first of these times of prayer has frequently taken one of two forms: a prayer for openness to God's presence (what we will call simply Opening Prayer) or a prayer of confession.

The *Opening Prayer* acknowledges the presence of God with the worshiping community and asks that those gathered may be receptive to the spirit, word, and action of God in the service. A brief prayer like the following can be offered in unison or by the worship leader.

4   Almighty God, we come seeking you
     in the midst of our joy and our brokenness,
     as individuals and as a community.
     Move among us during this hour of worship.
     By the power of your Holy Spirit,
     turn us from our foolishness to your truth
     in our thoughts, prayers and songs,
     and in all our living.
     For we pray in the name of Jesus Christ. Amen.

Because the opening prayer has often been understood "to invoke" God's presence in the service, it has frequently been called the "prayer of invocation." In this book, however, the term "invocation" is being used for the part of the communion prayer which invokes the presence of the Holy Spirit in the communion meal.

The *Prayer of Confession* is a corporate prayer which acknowledges both individual and communal transgression, both our guilt before God and our failure as church to live up to our vocation as the body of Christ. It includes an expression of sorrow for sins of commission and omission as well as a plea for the forgiveness which is promised by the death and resurrection of Christ. The prayer may include a promise or resolution by the penitent to live more closely conformed to the will of God.

Although it has been common practice for Disciples to incorporate the confession of sin into the pastoral prayer, it is increasingly common—especially during Advent and Lent—to find the Prayer of Confession set apart from the pastoral prayer, either near the beginning of the service or as a part of the preparation for communion. At the beginning of worship, prayerful confession frees worshipers to hear and respond to God's Word with unburdened, grateful hearts. Later in the service, worshipers are brought to confession by the impact of the Word of God which they have just heard. Since persons need to express their sin, it is appropriate for the prayer to be said in unison or as a litany between congregation and worship leader.

When a Prayer of Confession is offered, it is followed by *Words of Assurance*. The purpose of these words, which are ordinarily spoken by a worship leader, is to assure the congregation that by the grace of God and through faith and repentance they are released from bondage to sin. By saying the Words of Assurance, usually based on scripture, the leader reminds the community that forgiveness is through Jesus Christ who is our hope and salvation. Thus the congregation could pray and be assured in a pattern such as the following:

5   **Prayer of Confession**
    Holy God of steadfast love,
    have mercy upon us,
    for we are a warring, strife-torn people.
    Forgive us our greed, our envy,
    our hatred and suspicion, our betrayals,
    our lack of love and joy.

We ask from you the forgiveness
that we so often do not extend to one another.
In your great mercy, hear our prayer.
Pardon and deliver us from all our sins,
and grant us peace. Amen.

Words of Assurance
"The saying is sure and worthy of full acceptance.
Christ Jesus came into the world to save sinners."
Friends, believe the Good News that comes from
God: In Jesus Christ we are forgiven.

(1 Timothy 1:15)

It is theologically appropriate to follow the Words of Assurance with an exchange of "peace." If placed at this point in the service, the *Peace* signifies our willingness to "forgive our debtors" even as we have been forgiven our debts. It is also appropriate, however, to exchange words and gestures of reconciliation (peace) in the context of the Lord's Supper. If both an opening prayer and a prayer of confession are used at the beginning of the service, the former could be placed after the greeting and before the hymn in order to avoid an awkward succession of prayers. A few seconds of silence immediately preceding and following the prayers, no matter where they occur in the order of worship, will allow the congregation to bring its full attention to the act of prayer.

THE COMMUNITY PROCLAIMS THE WORD OF GOD

In biblical tradition, the Word is the active power by which God accomplishes the divine purpose. When God speaks, the world is created, judgment falls, salvation comes. The Word becomes flesh. Thus, today, when we speak of the Word of God, we refer not to the Bible alone but to the creating, judging, sustaining word which is spoken afresh, thus taking flesh anew in every generation. While this Word addresses the world in many ways, it customarily finds expression during worship in the readings from the Bible and in the sermon, and it is enacted in the meal at the Lord's table.

Prayer for Illumination
The proclamation of the Word of God may begin with a *Prayer for Illumination*. This brief prayer, which may also be the opening prayer, asks God through the Holy Spirit to empower us so that our reading and preaching may become the living, contemporary

Word of God for the congregation, that the people may be open and receptive to that Word, and that the congregation may respond to this encounter by faithfully living that Word in the world.

6   O God, prepare the soil of our hearts
    so that as your Word is sown
    through reading and preaching
    it may take root, mature,
    and come to harvest in the life of the world.
    Through Jesus Christ, the sower of the seed. Amen.

Readings from the Bible

The public reading of the scriptures reminds the church that we have inherited a tradition which has its roots in God's promises to Abraham and Sarah. The Bible reveals the character of God and the nature of God's creating, redeeming, and sustaining activity in the world. It shows us that we are sinners, redeemed by grace and empowered by the Holy Spirit. Scripture causes us to remember that the redemptive work of God is still unfinished; indeed, the whole cosmos waits for "a new heaven and a new earth." The Bible serves as a model not only for discerning the presence, power, and purpose of God, but also for discerning the role of the church in the continuing work of God in the world.

The practice of multiple readings from the Bible in a single service is rooted in the synagogue. Early in its life, the church found the meaning of its life interpreted by the Hebrew Scriptures.[3] As the writings of the apostolic period became normative for the church, the church also read from them, reminding itself in public worship of the good news of what God had done and continued to do through Jesus Christ.

Thus, for the church, the three readings represent the full history of salvation. They remind us that the God of Jesus and the church is also the God who created the world, delivered Israel from bondage, and spoke through the prophets. In recent times, the Hebrew Scriptures have been neglected in the life of the church. In order to help restore our Jewish heritage to the memory and experience of the Christian community, the reading from the Hebrew Scriptures should be retained, even if only two lessons from the Bible are read on a particular Sunday. (For a discussion of the principles of selection and a table of Bible readings, see pp. 172-191).

In order to dramatize the close connection between the Bible and the sermon, as well as to keep the scripture lessons freshly in the mind of the congregation, the lessons should be read in close proximity to the preaching. Scripture can, of course, stand on its own; a sermon need not "tie together" all three readings. If one of the selections is not read as a lesson, it can still be used in the service, for example, as a basis for the communion meditation or call to worship.

The public reading of scripture is often as flat as an airless balloon. Readers need to prepare carefully, paying close attention to the mood of the passages, to words and phrases which need to be accented, and to the pace and timing of the reading. For the hearing impaired, as well as for those who do not carry Bibles with them to worship, provision for a printed copy of the scripture lessons is helpful.

Response to the Readings

The importance of the reading is underlined and its impact strengthened if the reader or congregation makes an immediate response. Perhaps the response most common to Disciples is a request for the blessing of God on the reading, as in the familiar, "May God bless to our understanding the reading of this Holy Word." The response could also be a statement of thanksgiving: "Thanks be to God for this reading from the Holy Word"; or it could be an affirmation like that of Isaiah 40:8:

7   The grass withers,
     the flower fades,
     but the word of our God
     will stand forever.

Another response is a brief *dialogue* of affirmation and thanksgiving:

8   Leader   This is the Word of the Lord!
     People   Thanks be to God!

Some texts invite a response simply of *silence* and contemplation.

The reading from the Hebrew Scriptures is frequently followed by a *Psalm*. Throughout Christian history psalms have been sung. Protestants are best acquainted with metrical translations sung as hymns, such as "All People That on Earth Do Dwell," translated from Psalm 100. New patterns for singing nonmetrical psalms are being used with increasing frequency. Psalms may also be recited responsively. When not used at this point in the service, the psalm could be adapted as a call to worship or as a litany. Many of the psalms and psalm portions used in this book are taken from a new translation that is described on pages 154.

A trinitarian response of praise is sometimes used in order to glorify the God who in three Persons, is the beginning and the end, the creator and preserver, the one who has become flesh as the living Word, Jesus Christ. The most familiar trinitarian ascription is the "Gloria Patri." A congregation could also use a verse of a hymn such as the following adaptation of "Come, Thou Almighty King":

9 To thee, great One in three
   Eternal praises be
   Hence ever more.
   Thy sovereign majesty
   May we in glory see,
   And to eternity
   Love and adore.

Other hymns which lift up the Word of God work well as responses. For instance, verses from hymns such as "O Word of God Incarnate" or "O Grant Us Light that We May Know" can be used effectively.

The gospel reading is sometimes followed by affirmation and praise for the special place of the gospel in the life of the church.

10 Leader   This is the gospel of the Lord.
    People   Praise to you, Lord Jesus Christ.

An *Anthem* or other vocal music may be sung during the service of the Word since both the spoken word and the sung word can interpret the scriptural readings. The anthem may also be used elsewhere in the service, as an act of prayer, as a confession of faith or of sin, as part of the offering, or as part of the liturgy of the Lord's Supper.

A brief *Sermon for Children* may be inserted after one of the readings. This form of the Word of God expresses the unity of young and old in God's providential care. By presenting the Gospel at a level appropriate to their understanding, it helps children feel that they are full partners in the people of God. Its purpose is not the entertainment of adults, but the relating of the Gospel (perhaps with the help of visual aids or simple activities) to the lives of children.

Sermon

The roots of preaching are as old as the need for the meaning of life to be made more comprehensible. Since the time of Israel, each new generation of the people of God has required that the significance of its relation to God and of its history, identity, and mission be interpreted. What is the importance of the exodus from Egypt to those who are in exile in Babylon? How are we to understand God's gift and promise of Christian unity given our current separation from one another? Where is the new heaven and the new earth for those who live in bitter poverty?

In a sense, preaching is the interpretation of life in the light of God and the interpretation of God in the light of life. Preaching states the clear and compelling claim of the Gospel on the life of the congregation and the world. In an age confused by competing values, experiences, and sources of power and meaning, the sermon helps the congregation to discern and to respond faithfully to those things that are of God. The sermon identifies the action of God and shows how that action renews our life today.

Ordinarily the sermon is fed by four sources. (1) The scriptures are the fundamental and generative witness to the presence, purpose, and power of God in the world. (2) The tradition of the church brings us into conversation with Christians of other times and places and with their understandings of God. (3) Contemporary experience in the world at large and within the Christian community verifies and challenges the claims of scripture and tradition. Put negatively, we cannot divorce our reading of scripture and tradition from the experiences that make us who we are in the present. Put positively, true preaching occurs when, through faithful proclamation and receptive attention, the God to whom the Bible testifies engages us in the midst of our experience here and now. (4) The responsible exercise of reason brings together scripture, tradition and experience with modern understandings of reality. The claims of a given text or doctrine, and even of the Gospel itself, are evaluated according to modern notions of what is intelligible. By the same token, reason helps us see how the gospel challenges the adequacy of contemporary understandings of the world.

The fundamental work of preaching is to declare the good news of God to the congregation in such a way that the people will want joyfully to embrace it. This is no time for easy moralizing or passing out helpful hints on living, but for declaring the Gospel and providing ways in which people can respond to it. A sermon should not simply "explain" a text but embody the reality to which the text points, allowing the congregation to enter into that reality. For example, if the text is one of forgiveness, the preacher will want the congregation to understand the nature of forgiveness, to feel forgiven, and to forgive. In this sense, preaching has a sacramental quality: it mediates grace.

A sermon that is intellectually compelling, emotionally powerful, personally touching, and socially sensitive can move the congregation to greater intensity of participation in the other parts of the worship service. No matter how carefully prepared and delivered, however, the sermon cannot make up for a crudely conceived liturgy, just as the most eloquent liturgy is undermined by impoverished preaching.

THE COMMUNITY RESPONDS TO THE WORD OF GOD

Call to Discipleship
The Word of God begets a response. During worship, we represent the full response, which is all of life given to God, through symbolic gestures and statements. For many Disciples, the first liturgical response to the Word is the *Call to Discipleship*, sometimes called *"The Invitation,"* which offers five opportunities to the congregation: (1) Those who have never made a confession of faith and have never been baptized may make such a confession and indicate their desire to be baptized by coming to the front of the church (often while a "Hymn of Discipleship" is being sung).[4] (2) The Call to Discipleship is also an opportunity for those who are seeking a new congregational home to transfer their fellowship into the congregation and to receive public welcome. (3) At this time, people who were baptized at a very young age may make their own affirmation of baptismal vows and thus enter more fully into the life of the congregation. (4) Others may wish publicly to reaffirm their faith, to recommit themselves to faithful witness, or to offer grateful testimony to God and the church for blessings which they have received. (5) Still others may use the time privately to rededicate their lives in faith and service.

Affirmation of Faith

Affirmations of faith, sometimes called creeds (from the Latin word credo, "I believe"), summarize the faith of the people of God and have been used in Jewish and Christian worship from the biblical era. The affirmation from Deuteronomy 6, "Hear, O Israel, the Lord our God is one Lord" is central to every Sabbath service in the synagogue. The earliest Christian confessions or affirmations were probably statements of belief given by the church to candidates for baptism (e.g., 1 Corinthians 12:3 and Acts 8:37). By the third century these had developed into the confession known as the Apostles' Creed. Still later came those confessions—most notably the Nicene Creed—which were issued by councils of the church as part of the effort to define the church's faith in the midst of controversy. The Nicene Creed became a regular part of the eucharistic liturgy in the eleventh century, and has continued to be used by most Christian traditions down to our day.

Several branches of North American Protestantism, including the Disciples, developed an anti-credal position, objecting strenuously to the use of credal documents such as the *Westminster Confession* as tests of fellowship. Used as guardians of orthodoxy, creeds create barriers to Christian life and mission; and they cause controversy and division. When used as witnesses to Christian faith, especially in a day like our own when vigorous study of the Bible and the history and beliefs of the church is not widespread, a liturgical affirmation of faith can remind the congregation of the distinctive and essential witness of the Christian community. The reciting of the two ancient Christian confessions is a strong sign of the unity that ties the church together across the generations and cultures.

By making an affirmation of faith, believers confess God as the fundamental reality of their lives and acknowledge that the triune God—Father, Son, and Holy Spirit, to use the technical language of the church—is the source of their salvation and of their unity as followers of Christ. The Affirmation thus links the contemporary community with Christians in every time and place who have found their salvation in God. A contemporary creed can interpret the ancient faith for modern times. The *Preamble to the Design of the Christian Church (Disciples of Christ)*, for example, uses contemporary language to rehearse the witness of the church through the centuries, and thus is an appropriate response to the proclamation of the Word.

Certain passages of scripture may be used as affirmations of faith. Philippians 2:6-11, Ephesians 4:4-6 and 1 Timothy 3:16 are examples of texts that commend themselves as responses to the Word, as does the following passage from Mark 12:29-31:

11   Leader   Let us affirm our faith as Christians.
      People   **"The first commandment is this:**
      Hear, O Israel, the Lord your God is the only Lord.
      Love the Lord your God with all your heart,
      with all your soul, with all your mind,
      and with all your strength.
      The second is this:
      Love your neighbor as yourself.
      There is no other commandment
      greater than these."

Prayers of the People

The prayers of the people form a significant response to the gracious initiative of God, proclaimed in scripture and through preaching. This special period of focused, communal praying is shaped by our understanding of the nature of God. Through Christ we have come to know God as the source of comfort and new life, as Parent—both Father and Mother to us in life's deepest experiences. Therefore we dare to pour out before God our deepest joys and concerns as a community of faith. Such prayer is not an expression of *individual* need or personal thanksgiving (though it may encompass these), but a *corporate* response to the One who has given us life, redeemed us, and called us into being as mutually responsible members of one body. To put it another way, the prayers we offer in worship are not extensions or accumulations of individual prayer; rather, the prayers we offer in private are extensions or partial expressions of the corporate prayer which finds its fullest voice in these moments of public worship.

The period of prayer may take one of several forms. The most familiar is probably the traditional *pastoral prayer*, a single prayer offered by the pastor (or other worship leader) on behalf of the people. Other forms include *short prayers* delivered by different members of the congregation, a *litany* spoken by leader and congregation, or a *bidding prayer* in which the leader bids the congregation to pray silently or aloud for a series of things, naming them one at a time and following each with a period of silence. A leader may also lead the congregation in *guided meditation* inviting them to meditate prayerfully on images of God and of life broken and restored. In the course of any form of prayer, a time could be provided for members of the congregation to speak aloud their thanksgivings, intercessions and petitions.

A responsive prayer form gives the congregation verbal participation. At natural breaks in the prayer, the leader offers a stylized line which alerts the congregation to respond aloud. A traditional form is:

12   Leader   God, in your mercy,
     People   Hear our prayer.

The prayer period may begin with the gathering of requests for prayer during which the leader invites other worshipers to name their joys and concerns (but not to make general announcements). In some congregations, members who have special prayers to offer are invited to stand or kneel at the Lord's table along with elders who may pray with them, silently or aloud. The leader can help the congregation call to mind specific themes related to the season of the church year, or name major items of public interest (e.g., threats to peace and human dignity around the world). As a part of this period, the worship leader can also state items of pastoral interest, such as births, weddings, anniversaries, illnesses, and deaths. These statements provide content for silent prayer and may be referred to in the spoken prayer which follows. Provision for silence during the period of prayer is important as it allows worshipers to center upon God and to offer their own prayers in the context of the gathered community.

When the prayer is offered by one person, he or she must prepare carefully so that these words become truly a prayer of the people and not a mini-sermon directed from the leader to the people. In order to emphasize the corporate character of the prayer, the leader should generally avoid the use of "I" in favor of "we." Specific, concrete, evocative language and imagery in the prayer will lead the members of the congregation to pray out of the specific and concrete realities of their own lives.

The concerns of Christian prayer go far beyond the walls of the congregation. The congregation will want to pray for the global church, for the whole world which "God so loved" and for which Jesus died. In this way the church not only establishes its solidarity with the wider Christian community but exercises its servant ministry by praying on behalf of those who may not even know to call upon the name of God.

Prayer can be introduced by a hymn which establishes a mood in concert with the tone of the prayer, frequently quiet and meditative, though sometimes more exuberant. The time of prayer may begin by singing from memory stanzas of familiar hymns or scripture choruses.

Discussions of prayer frequently lift up six components of Christian spirituality which, when combined, form a flexible pattern for public prayer: (1) an opening address of praise and adoration, (2) confession, (3) thanksgiving, (4) intercession, (5) petition, and (6) a closing statement of submission.

Address of Praise and Adoration: When we pray we talk to God. The title or name of God that we use at the beginning of the prayer is marked by expressions of adoration, by a movement away from ourselves and toward the Great Shepherd, the Source of all goodness, the Light of our days. We praise God, lifting up particular aspects of God's being, power and activity, thereby indicating how God is encountered anew in worship and life.

Confession: If the service does not already include a time of confession, the prayer of the people is a needed opportunity to pour out our alienation, to confess our failures, and to seek restoration.

Thanksgiving: Prayer expresses our gratitude for the countless gifts flowing over us. Remembering these gifts is one way of rehearsing holy history, for we give thanks to the same God who liberated Israel, heard Mary and Martha's prayer for their brother's life, and bestowed the Spirit on the community in Jerusalem. Such thanksgiving, as Psalm 50 observes, is the richest sacrifice we can place before the God Most High.

Intercession: Intercession is the very heart of the community's prayer. The congregation, with confidence in the sovereignty and love of God, prays for those beyond its boundaries, for those who are broken and suffering, for those who especially need the guidance of God. Intercession is an act of communal self-giving, an act of participation in the healing, reconciling mission of God, and, as such, is an important part of the church's own mission in and for the world.

Petition: In the same way, the congregation brings before God its own needs and concerns, praying particularly that it may be strengthened to live in accordance with God's will. Petitionary prayer is sometimes dismissed as a selfish projection of human desires (despite the fact that the Lord's Prayer is a series of petitions). At its best, petitionary prayer is not self-seeking but self-dedicating to the One who enjoined us to "ask," "knock," "seek."

Submission: In most Protestant worship, prayer is offered not to Jesus but to God in the name of Jesus (in line with the injunction of John 14:14). In biblical thought, "to call upon the name" is to invoke the power of the one named. Thus, to pray in the name of Jesus is to pray in the power of the resurrection and with confidence in the One who raised Jesus from the dead. To pray in the name of Jesus is also to submit the prayer of the community to the will of the living Savior. And, as the prayer is submitted to the will of God, so the life of the congregation is submitted to that will. Prayer must involve a commitment to participate with God in the realization of that for which the community has prayed.

It is important to stress that all six of these elements need not find expression in every prayer, though the worship service as a whole should certainly contain them.

THE COMMUNITY COMES TOGETHER
AROUND THE LORD'S TABLE

The response of thankful praise reaches its climax in the Lord's Supper. The table is set with gifts that represent the mystery of the gospel: Jesus' body and blood offered on the cross for us, and our bodies offered to God as our spiritual worship (see Romans 12:1-2).

The basic form of the communion service is shaped by the institution narratives of scripture. On the night before his death Jesus (1) took the bread and cup, (2) gave thanks over them, (3) broke the bread, and (4) gave the bread and cup to the disciples to eat and drink. These four actions continue to outline the communion service, with minister, elders and deacons, and members of the congregation doing all essential parts. The lifting up of the bread and wine become the offering, with the people of the church sharing in the act that Jesus himself performed on the night when this supper was instituted. Jesus' prayer is offered by the ministers and elders, with the full membership encouraged to join at designated places. A leader breaks the bread and the elements are distributed to the deacons who serve the congregation. Then in this feast of life the communion with God and one another is renewed. These basic actions are celebrated with music, prayer, and ceremony that express its religious depth and power.

Invitation to the Lord's Table

The communion service itself begins with an invitation extended to the congregation on behalf of the true host, Jesus Christ. Often called the *communion meditation*, the invitation takes the form of a brief statement of the meaning of communion and uses that theme as the basis for inviting baptized Christians to come to this table. As explained below, the offering may be considered the beginning of the communion service. The invitation would then include a summons to offer gifts of praise and thanksgiving:

13 At this table we give thanks to God for the gifts that only God can give—life itself, the new life in Jesus Christ, and all of the supporting provisions that sustain us. Let us therefore prepare the table with our gifts, taken from life; and then by word and action praise the one who cares for us so richly.

The Offering

The offering, a central act of worship, is both a thankful response to the proclamation to the Word of God and an act of preparation for the Lord's Supper. The offering of money, or other material possessions, is a way of confessing that all we have comes from God and of signifying our intent to be thankful stewards of God's creation. In keeping with biblical precedents, these gifts are used for the support of the church and its mission in the world (for example, 2 Corinthians 8:1-7; Acts 11:27-30). Like the bread and wine, the material offerings are commended to God for God's transforming use.

It is increasingly common for the elements of communion to be carried to the Lord's table with the offering of money. The offering of bread and cup signifies that God comes to us in this meal through the simple gifts and labors of our everyday lives and reminds us that the meal itself is a thankful response to the unique, immeasurable sacrifice of Christ—the one true offering. The time of collection is appropriate for an offering of music or dance, praising our Creator with the special talents given to members of the community.

A hymn of thanksgiving or dedication may be sung while the offering, including the loaf and the cup, is brought to the table. Hymns such as "Take My Life and Let It Be," "Love Divine, All Loves Excelling," "We Place upon Your Table, Lord," and "Now Thank We All Our God" are examples. The "Doxology" may also be used at this point. A verse by Isaac Watts, set to the tune usually used with "All Creatures of Our God and King" (*Lasst uns erfreuen*) serves this function very well.

14   From all that dwell below the skies
Let the creator's praise arise.
Alleluia, alleluia.
Let the redeemer's name be sung
Through ev'ry land, in ev'ry tongue.
Alleluia, alleluia,
Alleluia, alleluia, alleluia.

The offering is followed by the communion prayers which include the meaning of self-dedication. Thus a separate offertory prayer can be omitted, allowing the congregation's sung response to stand as a sufficient act of dedication.[5]

Prayers at the Table—Their Meaning

The most highly developed part of the Lord's Supper, and the most important set of words in the service, is the act of giving thanks, the communion (or eucharistic) prayer. Here the church expresses in words spoken to God the meaning of these actions with bread, wine, and our other offerings.

The communion prayer is shaped not only by the actions that surround it but also by the threefold nature of God's self revelation. It begins by giving thanks to God whom the ancient creeds affirm as "Maker of heaven and earth," whom Jesus calls "Abba, Father," and whom Christians of every time and place experience as mysterious presence and power. Often this part of the prayer recites God's marvelous work of giving life, calling us to be a special people, and saving us from sin.

The communion prayer then changes its focus to the second way that God is known in Christian faith. We remember Jesus Christ who as Word of God was present at creation and was spoken of by prophets. The prayer remembers that when the time was right Jesus emptied himself, took the form of a servant, and came to live among us. The remembrance of Jesus reaches its climax when we recall his death on the cross for our salvation and his rising from the grave by the power of God.

As a result of biblical scholarship over the past half century, it now is generally agreed that remembrance or memorial, when set in the context of proclamation, thanksgiving, and invocation of the Holy Spirit, has a special meaning. Remembrance is not to be understood only as a mental recollection of an event that happened "back then" and "over there," but as an action whereby the reality of God's saving act in Christ is made newly present for each generation. Our prayer at the communion table is that through the power of the Holy Spirit Christ will become present to us in the breaking of bread and drinking from the cup.

Because the communion prayer combines the praise of God and the remembering of God's saving work in Jesus Christ, it has traditionally included the biblical words of institution. These words have been handed down to us as the words of Jesus himself. When made a part of our conversation with God at the communion table, they connect us even more intimately with Jesus and the disciples gathered around him in the upper room.[6]

The communion prayer then focuses on the third way that God is known by asking the Holy Spirit to move in a special way in the service of communion. This part of the prayer is sometimes called the *Invocation*, which is based on a Latin word, or *Epiclesis*, based on a Greek word, both words meaning "to call upon." The prayer asks that the Spirit act in bread and wine and the congregation so that the sacrifice of Christ becomes a real part of our lives, a living presence, here and now. It asks, too, that through participation in this meal the community of the faithful may be changed and empowered by God's spirit, that we may become what we celebrate: the one body of Christ given for the world. God takes the life of the community, blesses it with the gift of Christ through the supper, breaks it and gives it for service in the world. Our thanksgiving for the gifts of God is empty rhetoric if there is no intention of self-giving, no commitment to live eucharistically (i.e., thankfully), no commitment to overcome the barriers of race, class and confession that divide the human family.[7]

Prayers at the Table—Their Form
Early in the history of the church, the communion prayer assumed a definite form that is continued today in most Catholic and Protestant churches around the world. The standard components of this prayer include:
—an introductory dialogue ("Lift up your hearts") which establishes the dominant theme of thanksgiving;
—an expression of joyful praise and thanksgiving for God's saving activity through creation (frequently, though misleadingly, called a "preface");
—a congregational response, usually the "sanctus" ("Holy, Holy, Holy Lord . . .") and, in some churches, the "benedictus" ("Blessed is he who comes in the name of the Lord . . .");

—the scriptural words of institution which recall that it was Jesus who instituted this rite and proclaimed its meaning;
—a memorial in which we remember Christ's life, death, and resurrection; and rejoice in what he has done and is doing for our salvation;
—an invocation of the Holy Spirit in which we pray for the presence of God's Spirit on the loaf and cup and on the gathered congregation;
—a doxology and amen.

This type of prayer is illustrated in the following example which draws upon the Preamble to the *Design of the Christian Church (Disciples of Christ)*. Other examples can be found in the service books of most other churches.

15   *Dialogue*
The Lord be with you.
And also with you.
Lift up your hearts.
We lift them to the Lord.
Let us give thanks to the Lord our God.
It is right to give our thanks and praise.

Preface
Holy God, with one voice
we offer you our thankful praise.
We rejoice that you are God,
maker of heaven and earth
and of the covenant of love
which binds us to you and to one another.
With the church of all times and places
we lift our voices in thankful praise.

Sanctus
Holy, holy, holy Lord,
God of power and might!
Heaven and earth are full of your glory.
Hosanna in the highest!

Institution
In the fullness of time,
you sent your Son, Jesus Christ,

to be our Lord and the Savior of the World.
On the night when he was betrayed
Jesus took bread,
and when he had given thanks,
he broke it, and said,
"This is my body which is given for you.
Do this in remembrance of me."
In the same way he took the cup
after supper, saying,
"This cup is the new covenant in my blood.
Do this as often as you drink it,
in remembrance of me."

Christ has died,
Christ is risen,
Christ will come again!

Memorial
At this table, Holy God,
we celebrate with thanksgiving
the saving acts and presence of Christ.
By his ministry among the poor and forgotten
you teach us your gracious compassion.
By his death on the cross
you show your suffering love.
By his resurrection from the silent tomb
you display your glorious power.
By his promise to return
you offer us endless hope.
Come, Lord Jesus, come!

Invocation
We thank you God, Fountain of life,
for this bread and cup.
Grant that by the power of your Holy Spirit
we who receive them
may share in the body and blood
of our Savior Jesus Christ.
Fill us with this same Spirit
that we may be given power for our mission
of witness and service to all people.
Come, Holy Spirit, come!

Doxology
In the bonds of Christian faith
we yield ourselves to you, O God,
that we may serve the One
whose rule among us has no ending.

**Blessing, glory, and honor
be yours forever! Amen.**

Many Disciples, acknowledging the power and beauty of the historic form, use prayers following that pattern on special occasions. For normal Sunday use, however, most Disciples use another form of prayer at the communion table. This second type of communion prayer assigns responsibility for developing its language and structure to the congregation and its leaders, using ideas that the leader has prepared to offer on this occasion. This form of communion prayer values simplicity, flexibility, and spontaneity.

In many Disciples congregations, there are two short communion prayers, often called prayers for the loaf and for the cup. Even here, as the following examples illustrate, the classic themes can be incorporated into this form that is traditional among Disciples.

16 A Prayer for the Loaf
Eternal God, we offer thanks
for the gift of bread,
the sign of all your provisions for us.
By bread you nourish our life,
bring us pleasure, and
bind us into communities of love.
Even more we praise you for this
bread of communion by which,
through the power of your Spirit,
you make present Jesus' own body
given for us.
Eternal God, Source of Life,
all praise is yours. Amen.

17 A Prayer for the Cup
Merciful God, we praise you
for this cup of blessing

which brings us the new life
that comes from you.
Even though we go against your will,
you do not condemn us,
but offer forgiveness and
the power to do better.
As we drink from this cup,
unite us with Jesus
whose blood of the covenant was poured out
so that we could be forgiven.
Empower us with your Holy Spirit
to live the Christian life
faithfully and fully.
We offer these prayers in the name
of our Savior, Jesus Christ. Amen.

Prayers at the Table—Enlarging Disciples' Practice

A distinctive mark of worship in the Christian Church (Disciples of Christ) is the ministry in the Lord's Supper of lay elders who traditionally offer the communion prayers and deacons who distribute the elements to the congregation. It is also common practice for the pastor or other ordained minister of the church to share in leading communion. The minister's part has most frequently been a brief statement about the meaning of communion or an invitation to the table. The minister often breaks the bread ceremonially and recites the biblical words of institution. In most Disciples' churches, the congregation sings a communion hymn but has no other speaking role in the administration of the Lord's Supper.

Thankful Praise recommends that the customary practice of Disciples be enlarged in order to strengthen the theological and devotional content of the service and to provide for fuller participation by minister and congregation.

The first recommendation is that the people's part in communion be expressed more fully by framing the communion prayer (or prayers) with two elements in which the congregation also speaks: at the beginning of the prayer, the classical dialogue; and at the close, the Lord's Prayer. The dialogue, which has often been called the *Sursum corda* (the Latin for "Lift Up Your Hearts,"), is given in the prayer on page 148 and appears in some of the other prayers in this book. This responsive element is always appropriate as the beginning of the communion prayer.

While the Lord's Prayer may come earlier in the service, it is particularly appropriate following the other prayers at the Lord's table; the communion prayers lead naturally to the climax provided by the greatest of all Christian prayers. The eschatological language of the Lord's Prayer (e.g., "your kingdom come") reinforces the important connection between the eucharist and the time when the whole universe will be conformed to the will of God. Our prayer is that the joy we experience at this table will come to pass for all creation. A translation in modern English has been developed by the Consultation on Common Texts and is now appearing in new books of services and prayers:

18   Our father in heaven,
hallowed be your name,
your kingdom come,
your will be done,
on earth as in heaven.
Give us today our daily bread.
Forgive us our sins
as we forgive those
who sin against us.
Save us from the time of trial,
and deliver us from evil.
For the kingdom, the power,
and the glory are yours,
now and forever. Amen.

The second recommendation is that the communion prayers be clarified and strengthened by adding a portion said responsively by congregation and the pastor. This part of the prayer can bring out more fully the theological meaning of the service and the congregation's role as co-celebrants of communion. This responsive prayer can be used for several Sundays in succession, the Sundays of Advent or of Eastertide, for example. An example of this kind of responsive communion prayer is given below.

19   Pastor   Almighty and loving God,
you have created and redeemed us,
and through the presence of your Holy Spirit
you sustain us in daily life.

People   **Now let this same Spirit**
            descend upon these gifts
            that in the breaking of the bread
            and the sharing of this cup
            we may know the living presence of Jesus
            who gave his body and blood for all.

Pastor   May your Spirit fill us
            with a longing for deeper unity
            in Christ's body, the church,
            and with commitment to greater service
            in Christ's name in the world.

People   **Give us an unshakable hope**
            in the Holy Commonwealth
            which is to come.
            For we pray through Jesus Christ,
            with you and the Holy Spirit
            one God, now and forever. Amen.

The third recommendation is that the biblical Words of Institution of the Lord's Supper should always be included. They are recited either as the centerpiece of the prayer itself, or as the words declared while the bread is broken. Ecumenical usage would encourage that this portion of the communion service be said by an ordained minister of the church.[8]

The Breaking of the Bread

When the Prayers at the table have been completed, the bread is broken, following Jesus' own example. Many Disciples congregations have used matzos wafers as their communion bread, and these break with a clear snapping sound that intensifies the drama of this act of remembrance. Many congregations today use a small loaf of leavened bread, following ancient Christian practice. These loaves can be held high and broken so that all in the congregation can see. This part of the service can be done without audible words. If the Words of Institution were not included in the communion prayer, they can be recited as the bread is broken and the cup lifted up. Other words from scripture or later Christian tradition can be recited, either by the leader alone or with participation by the congregation, as in the following example drawn from 1 Corinthians 10.

20   Minister The bread which we break,
      **People   Is it not a participation
                  in the body of Christ?**
      Minister The cup of blessing which we bless,
      **People   Is it not a participation
                  in the blood of Christ?**
      Minister Because there is one bread,
                  we who are many are one body,
      People   For we all partake of the one bread.

The Peace

One way of symbolizing the reconciliation embodied in the Lord's Supper is for the presiding minister, following the prayers, to invite the congregation to share signs of peace: a visible greeting, a handshake, an embrace. The peace can also come at the beginning of the meal or immediately after the assurance of pardon.

A traditional verbal exchange accompanies the passing of the peace. The person giving says, "The peace of Christ be with you." The one receiving replies, "And also with you." The exchange may also occur between worship leader and people.

Communion

It is common practice in Disciples churches to distribute the bread and wine by passing plates and trays with individual cups to the seated congregation. In some congregations, the people eat the bread and drink from the cup as it is passed. When this practice is followed, members should recognize and, as far as possible, make visible that they are serving one another and not simply partaking in isolation. In other congregations, one or both of the elements are held until the entire congregation has been served. Then, at a signal from an elder or minister (for example, "Jesus said, 'This is my body; take, eat'"), the congregation communes together as a sign of common fellowship.

Still other congregations are discovering that the act of coming forward to receive a common loaf and cup is a powerful way of indicating that "because there is one bread, we who are many are one body" (1 Corinthians 10:17). Whatever the method of distribution, the period of communion should be a time of joyful reverence and meditation.

Prayer After Communion

This prayer is a thankful response to the Lord's Supper. In it we ask God to remind us again of the intimate bond between worship and mission, our participation at the Lord's table and our participation in the world. A prayer like the following may be offered by the pastor or an elder:

21 O God, we thank you
for uniting us by baptism
in the body of Christ
and by this meal filling us with joy and hope.
Grant that in the days ahead
our lips which have sung your praises
may speak the truth,
our eyes which have seen your love
may look with compassion
on the needs of the world,
our hands which have held
this loaf and cup
may be active in your service.
We ask it in the name of Jesus Christ. Amen.

THE COMMUNITY GOES FORTH TO SERVE GOD IN MISSION

Hymn

The last hymn sends forth the people with a sense of God's power and of their purpose in the world. The hymn often gives thanks for the redemption which has come to us in Christ, for the renewal which God gives us through participation in worship, or for the service we will render in the world.

Closing Words

The closing words in Christian worship have commonly been a *benediction* or *blessing* in the name of God. This is often combined with a *commission* to go forth to do God's work. The closing words often include a verse from scripture. Although these words sometimes are given as though they were a prayer, their proper form is a declaration of the favor of God which the worship leader addresses to the congregation. A classic blessing is Numbers 6:24-26:

22 The Lord bless you and keep you.
The face of the Lord shine upon you,
and be gracious to you.
The Lord look upon you with favor
and give you peace.

Closing Music

Once again the boundary between the sacred time of formal worship and "normal time" is usually indicated with music. Some members of the congregation may want to remain seated, reflecting on the experience of worship, until this music is completed. Others will move more quickly to a time of greeting and conversation. Such joyful fellowship is an appropriate extension of formal worship, a sign of the communion made possible by our common experience of grace through faith in Jesus Christ.

NOTES

1. Elsa Tamez, "Come Let us Celebrate" in *No Longer Strangers*, ed. Iben Gjerding and Katherine Kinnamon (Geneva: World Council of Churches, 1983) p. 20. Strong, vivid resources for worship are available in many collections, including resources that come from the church in other parts of the world, as does this call to communion.

2. Translation from Consultation on a Liturgical Psalter (Washington, D.C.: International Commission on English in the Liturgy, 1984). A fuller discussion of psalms in worship, excerpts from the ICEL project, and a table for the church year appear on pp. 154-171.

3. The sacred Scriptures of Protestant churches contain sixty-six books. It has been customary to refer to the first 39 books as the Old Testament and to the remainder as the New Testament. While it is helpful to be able to distinguish between these two bodies of literature, the designations "new" and "old" suggest discontinuity between the saving work of God in Israel and the church, as if the old were obsolete and invalid, having been replaced by the new. Modern theology and biblical scholarship, however, working in the awful memory of the Holocaust, are rediscovering the essential continuity of God's work from Abraham through Christ, the continuing validity of Judaism, and great commonality between the life and vocation of Israel and the life and vocation of the church. Seeking to express this common identity, yet honoring the integrity of Judaism and Christianity, *Thankful Praise* refers to the first 39 books of the Bible as the Hebrew Scriptures and the last 27 books as the Apostolic Writings.

4. The typical pattern in Disciples congregations is for the pastor to ask those who have come forward some variant of the following question: "Do you believe that Jesus is the Christ, the Son of the Living God, and do you take him as your Lord and Savior?" While such a formulation has the advantage of stating an intimate relationship between Jesus and the believer, it has at least two drawbacks: First, it opens the way for the saving work of Christ to be construed as an individualistic relationship with little regard for the corporate and cosmic dimensions of salvation. Second, it is the language of nineteenth-century revivalism and not of scripture. The Apostolic Writings speak more commonly of God our savior, God who "was in Christ reconciling the world to himself." A better practice would be for those responding to the "call" to repeat Peter's simple confession in Matthew 16:16: I believe that Jesus "is the Christ, the Son of the Living God." This affirmation links one with the great cloud of witnesses from every age who have confessed Jesus Christ.

5. The offering can also be understood without this direct connection to communion. It may, for example, become part of the response to the Word of God. The worship leader invites the congregation to participate in this act of *thanksgiving-through-offering*, usually by noting the biblical imperative for such an act. For example, the minister or an elder may say,

"As each has received a gift, employ it for one another, as good stewards of God's varied grace." Let us prepare the table for the sacred feast by bringing to it our offerings. (1 Peter 4:10)

Other suitable passages include Exodus 35:4b-5, Deuteronomy 16:16b-17, Psalm 96:6-8, Matthew 6:19-21, Luke 12:33-34, Acts 20:35, 2 Corinthians 8:9, and Hebrews 13:16.

The *Offertory Prayer* is a prayer, given by an elder or minister, dedicates not only our possessions but our very lives to God:

We give to you, O God, what is already yours
for all that we have is from your bounty.
Take our gifts, we pray,
and through us use them for your purposes
of peace, justice, and love.
Take our lives and shape them
that we may be instruments of your will.
Through Jesus Christ. Amen.

6. The four institution narratives are Matthew 26:26-29, Mark 14:22-25, Luke 22:14-19, and 1 Corinthians 11:23-26. One of these narratives should appear in every celebration of the Lord's Supper (indeed, many churches would not recognize the service as Holy Communion without these words). A recitation of Jesus' actual words, as we know them from scripture, is a basic part of the communion service. They remind us that he is the host, that this is not a performance of our contriving but a sacred act commanded of us by our Lord.

7. Something about a church's theological stance is inevitably revealed by the way this prayer relates the Holy Spirit, the bread and wine, Christ's body and blood, and the worshiping community. What is being requested? What is understood to take place? Disciples today generally resist a well-defined position, arguing that the mystery of the Spirit's operation precludes dogmatic answers and instead depends on theological (and liturgical) diversity. This means that between the extremes of transubstantiation and historical remembrance there is a wide range of liturgical formulations that can be used. Each of the following examples implies a slightly different theological orientation.

—May your Holy Spirit descend upon us and upon these gifts, showing them to be holy gifts for a holy people, the bread of life and the cup of salvation.

—Send your Holy Spirit that through these gifts we might be filled with new life in Christ Jesus.

—Grant that by the power of your Holy Spirit these gifts of bread and wine might be for us his body and his blood.

—May your Spirit fill us anew, through this act of holy remembrance, with the real and saving presence of Christ.

—May the power of the Holy Spirit accomplish the words of your Son who said "This is my body; this is my blood."

8. It is appropriate that the Words of Institution be said by an ordained minister. Disciples reject the idea that the "validity" of the meal depends on whether or not the person who presides at the table is "properly" ordained; but there are good reasons, nevertheless, for making this our normal practice: (1) Ordained ministers have always signified the unity and continuity of Christ's church. An ordained presider reminds the local congregation that it is joined to Christians of all times and places around this holy table. (2) We set apart persons for ministry of word and sacrament, not to make them a separate caste but precisely in order that they may represent to the church its own mission and identity (especially at central moments of the church's life such as communion). To insist that there be lay persons presiding in order "to represent laity" is to imply a contrary understanding of ordination. (3) Ecumenical partners are telling Disciples that this is an issue of great importance to the larger Christian community. As Disciples participate in the Consultation on Church Union and other ecumenical dialogues we are finding that our commitment to the one true church of Christ is more fully expressed when we include the pastor along with the elders as one of the leaders of communion.

THE SEASONS OF ADVENT AND CHRISTMAS

Advent is a complex season of ironies and contrasts. It is a festal season, celebrating the human birth of Jesus in a Judean village; yet it is also a penitential season in which we examine and prepare ourselves for his promised return, including his Second Coming in glory and judgment. It is a time for remembering the first witnesses to God's incarnation in Jesus of Nazareth; yet it is also a time for acknowledging that Christ is born ever anew in our midst, and that we, too, bear witness to the miracle. It is the time of year when the sun, for those in the Northern Hemisphere, sinks to its lowest point on the horizon; yet in such wintry darkness we give thanks for the birth of the Son who is, we confess, the light of the world.

The ironies increase. Advent is a season of waiting and anticipation, though the church has long recognized that the waiting itself brings fulfillment. Advent is a period for emphasizing hope and expectation, though ours is surely an active hope that demands committed discipleship to the Prince of Peace here and now. The very placement of the season is ironic—and strangely appropriate. Coming at the end of the calendar year, Advent marks the beginning of the church's liturgical cycle. The birth narratives, found in the gospels of Matthew and Luke, set the stage for Christ's ministry and redemptive death, but we now know that these stories became part of the gospel tradition after the passion stories had taken root at the church's heart, just as Christmas was added to the liturgical calendar long after Easter and Holy Week were firmly established. The early Christians had first to confess Christ crucified and risen before they could understand the significance of Jesus' humble birth.

There are additional reasons why Advent, and the Christmas celebration which is its culmination, is a challenging season for those with responsibility for community worship. The stories of Jesus' birth are so well known that they can easily become clichés, obscuring the awesome message that God, the Holy One of Israel, has taken human form as a vulnerable child. North American Christians frequently carry a composite mental picture of a rough stable (more likely a cave in the Judean hillside) beneath a shining star, complete with donkey (never mentioned in the scriptural accounts), kings and shepherds (drawn from two different gospels), and hovering angels.

On the other hand, the fact that the stories are known at all means that the symbols, phrases, and concepts from these biblical narratives can be effectively used in worship as framework for interpreting our lives and the world in which we live them. In order for this to happen, however, Advent worship must recapture a sense of freshness. It must point beyond the pleasure of Christmas cards and presents to the true joy announced in Bethlehem. It must proclaim Emmanuel in a society unatuned to intimations of the eternal.

A Thematic Approach

Because Advent is a brief, four-week period, culminating in a major festival of the church, it lends itself as does no other season to focused thematic development. Here is a place where fresh approaches are certainly in order. For example, special attention could be given during each of the four weeks to scriptural figures whose joyful waiting for the Lord makes them models for us as we approach the Christmas event. One possible sequence, which could be modified in accordance with the lectionary, is the following:

Week 1: Elizabeth and Zechariah (Luke 1:68-79)
Week 2: John the Baptist (Luke 3:4-6)
Week 3: Anna and Simeon (Luke 2:29-32)
Week 4: Mary and Joseph (Luke 1:46-55)

Week 3, for instance, could use a call to worship and invocation similar to the following:

Call to Worship
23   "And there was a prophetess, Anna. She did not depart from
       the temple, worshiping with fasting and prayer night and

day. And [coming upon Simeon with the child Jesus] she gave thanks to God, and spoke of him to all who were looking for the redemption of Jerusalem." Anna, our ancestor in the faith, waited prayerfully for the coming of her Lord. In this same spirit, let us worship God.

Opening Prayer
24 As the Holy Spirit helped Simeon to know your presence in the infant Jesus, help us, dear God, to know your presence in the reading of scripture, the breaking of bread, and the friendship of this hour. Open our eyes to your salvation that we, too, may know your everlasting peace. Amen.

Another way of developing thematic coherence is to focus the prayers and readings for each week around the opening passages of a different gospel. The week devoted to Luke (by far the easiest and most obvious) could use the following kinds of materials:

Greeting
25 Blessed be the Lord God of Israel
who has visited and redeemed the people,
who has raised up a horn of salvation for us
in the house of the servant David,
who has performed the mercy promised to our ancestors
and remembered the holy covenant,
who has delivered us from the hand of our enemies
that we might serve God in holiness and righteousness
all the days of our lives.
(based on the Song of Zechariah, Luke 1:68-75)

Opening Prayer
26 God of our ancestors and our children,
we give you thanks for John the Baptist
and other prophets who went before Jesus
preparing his way and giving knowledge
of salvation to the people.
We pray that in this hour you will give
light to our darkness and guide our feet
in the way of peace.
Through Christ we pray. Amen.
(based on the Song of Zechariah, Luke 1:76-79)

Prayer at the Table

27   Leader   God of mercy and grace,
            Our souls declare your greatness
            and our spirits rejoice in you our Savior!
            You are mighty and do great things for your people.

    People   Holy is your name!
    Leader   You scatter the proud
            in the imaginations of their hearts,
            but have mercy on those who fear you.

    People   Holy is your name!
    Leader   You put down the mighty from their thrones,
            but exalt those of low degree.

    People   Holy is your name!
    Leader   You fill the hungry with good things,
            but the rich you send away empty.

    People   Holy is your name!
    Leader   God of love, we rejoice that
            when the time had come,
            you sent the Holy Child, Jesus, to be Emmanuel,
            your presence with us.
            He grew to be a teacher, a prophet, a servant,
            and in obedience to your will he became a victim
            freely accepting death on a cross
            that we might have life.
            With bread and wine we remember that
            on the night before his death, he took bread . . .

                                (based on the Song of Mary, Luke 1:46-55)

Closing Words

28   Let us now depart in peace, servants of our God, for our eyes
    have seen the salvation which God has prepared in the pres-
    ence of all people.

                                (based on the Song of Simeon, Luke 2:29-31)

    An alternative sequence is for these three songs (of Zechariah,
Mary, and Simeon) to be divided into litanies and used on three
Sundays of Advent. The fourth Sunday, in keeping with the
Lukan emphasis, could use a combination of Isaiah's hymn (repeat-
ed in Luke 3:4-6) and the Song of the Angels (Luke 2:14) as
follows:

29 Leader The voice of one crying in the wilderness:
Prepare the way of the Lord.
People Glory to God in the highest!
Leader Every valley shall be filled,
and every mountain and hill shall be brought low.
People Glory to God in the highest!
Leader The crooked shall be made straight,
and the rough ways shall be made smooth.
People Glory to God in the highest!
Leader All flesh shall see the salvation of God.
**All Glory to God in the highest,
and peace to God's people on earth!**

Lighting Advent Candles

During the past generation, many Protestant congregations have built their Advent worship around the themes of hope, peace, joy, and love. These services often include, immediately after the greeting, a time for lighting "Advent candles." During week one, for example, the "hope candle" could be lighted using the following words and actions:

Opening sentences
30 Leader Jesus Christ is the hope of the world.
People In God alone do we place our trust.

Hymn
During the singing of this hymn, the appropriate candle would be lighted, perhaps by representatives from the congregation. Other statements or ceremonies may be added, but this portion of the service should be kept brief, simple, and direct. Suggestions: "O God, Our Help in Ages Past," "All My Hope on God Is Founded," or "Hope of the World."

Special responsive readings can be developed around the particular theme for that week. The following declaration of hope is adapted from "A Common Account of Hope" written by the Faith and Order Commission of the World Council of Churches.

31 Leader 1 Advent is a time of hope as we await the birth of Jesus and the coming of the risen Christ. But the risen one is also the one who was crucified. This

reminds us that our life of hope is not a guarantee of safety, but an invitation to risk. To live in hope is never to have reached our goal, but always to be on a risk-laden journey.

People   **To live in hope is to risk affirming the new and reaffirming the old.**

Leader 2 Hope sends us on untried paths. When we lock ourselves to the past, we may grow deaf to the promptings of the Spirit. Yet the Spirit will ever reaffirm the truth of Christ who is the same yesterday, today, and forever. Hope embraces the risk of new departures and of faithfulness to the past.

People   **To live in hope is to risk self-criticism as the channel of renewal.**

Leader 1 Renewal arises as we are judged by God and led to a repentance that bears worthy fruit. Only those who can smile at themselves and their faults can be ultimately serious about other selves. Hope embraces the risk of self-criticism as the way to renewal.

People   **To live in hope is to risk dialogue.**

Leader 2 Genuine encounter with others demands vulnerability. It requires a willingness to explore new ways of stating God's truth. Because in dialogue we can receive a fuller understanding of our own faith and a deeper understanding of our neighbor, hope embraces the risk of dialogue.

People   **To live in hope is to risk struggle.**

Leader 1 Christians are denied the privilege of being "neither hot nor cold." We are called to confess our faith boldly, even when this means saying "no" to parts of the society in which we live. Hope embraces the risk of struggle.

People   **To live in hope is to risk scorn.**

Leader 2 To many of our contemporaries, our hope appears vain. To live in hope is nevertheless to continue to witness to the saving power of Jesus—"to give account of the hope that is in us"—whether we are ignored or attacked. Hope embraces the risk of ridicule.

People   **To live in hope is to risk death for the sake of that hope.**

Leader 1   Today Christians seldom face death for the sake of their faith, but genuine witness should still be costly. The Christian hope is not that death can be avoided, but that it can be overcome. Those who truly live in hope have come to terms with death and can risk dying with their Lord.

While the four traditional themes—hope, peace, joy and love—are certainly appropriate, they, too, can lose their freshness with overuse. Numerous alternatives are possible, including the following:

Week 1: Creation (associated with the birth of a child and loosely linked to the nativity narratives in John 1)
Week 2: Anticipation
Week 3: Revolution (made explicit in the Magnificat of Mary, Luke 1:46-55)
Week 4: Incarnation

Week 1, to give but one example, could incorporate the following as a responsive litany or prayer.

32   God of creation,
You gave us the gift of this earth—
with its minerals and waters,
with its flowers and fruits,
with its living creatures of grace and beauty,
that we might nurture them, stewards in your household.
Today we hear you ask:
What have you done to the water, the earth, the air?
Silence

God of love,
You gave us the gift of peoples—
of different races and colors,
of different customs and cultures,
of different opinions and points of view,
that we might share our lives, children in your household.
Today we hear you ask:
What have you done to your sister, your brother?
Silence

God of salvation,

You gave us the gift of your Son—
a child in Bethlehem,
a teacher in Galilee,
a suffering servant on the cross,
that we might follow him, members in the body of faith.
Today we hear you ask:
What have you done to the joy of Christmas and
the good news of Easter day?
Silence

Teach us, Creator, God of love and salvation, that the earth
and all its fullness . . . that the world and those who dwell
therein . . . that the church and all its parts . . . are yours. All
glory be to you now and forever. Amen.

Worship Resources for Advent and Christmas

Greetings

33   It is the season—
And we wait, tensed and listening
for the first sound of the promise, arrived.
Listen! Do you hear it?
The lusty cry of new life.
Emmanuel! God with us!
Hosanna in the highest!
Blessed be the name of the Lord!
Hosanna in the highest!

34   Christ comes to us like the the morning sun
on winter's snow,
blinding us with brilliance,
warming us through after the chill of night.
Welcome the Son!
Come, Lord Jesus

35   Watch and be ready!
The hour approaches.
Watch and be ready!
The time is at hand.
Watch and be ready!
Our Lord comes!

36   Leader   How beautiful upon the mountains
are the feet of one who brings good tidings;

People   **Who publishes peace and salvation,**
         Who says to Zion: "Your God reigns!"
Leader   The watchmen lift their voices,
         together they sing for joy.
People   **All the ends of the earth**
         shall see the salvation of our God.
                              (adapted from Isaiah 52:7-10)

Opening Prayers

37   God, our strength and our salvation,
     we live in dark times
     and desperately need your light.
     We carry a winter within us
     and desperately need your warmth.
     We turn neighbors into objects
     and desperately need your love.
     We raise money and power to the status of gods
     and desperately need your forgiveness.
     As we gather for this time of worship,
     fill us with the spirit of this season.
     In the wilderness of our world,
     send us as messengers to make straight
     a highway for our Lord,
     in whose name we pray. Amen.

38   O God, at this time of year when all of nature
     seems to reflect our despair and loneliness,
     the cry of Advent is heard throughout the land—
     the cry of holy expectation, the eternal hour of joy,
     the word of divine love.
     Be the word of hope to our despair,
     and help us to sing songs of joy. Amen.

39   Lord, you are coming
     and we confess that we are not ready!
     The place we provide for you is
     less than the roughest manger.
     The defenses we erect against you are
     greater than those of the worried king.
     By your loving presence in our lives, O God,
     make smooth the rough places in our hearts.
     Confound the defenses we have built.

Infect our wills with your goodness that we may
know Christ born anew in our midst and worship him.
Through Jesus Christ we pray. Amen.

40   God of hope and new birth,
We praise you for the promise of new light,
yet we ask: Why is there so much darkness?
We gave thanks for the birth of a child,
yet we ask: Why do so many children suffer?
We celebrate the gifts of magi and shepherds,
yet we ask: Why are the gifts of the earth
so unfairly divided?
Come, Lord Jesus!
Alone we are a hopeless people,
focused more on self than neighbor,
Come, Lord Jesus!
Come quickly! Amen.

Prayer of Confession
41   God we confess that ours is still a world
in which Herod seems to rule:
the powerful are revered,
the visions of the wise are ignored,
the poor are afflicted,
and the innocent are killed.
You show us that salvation comes
in the vulnerability of a child,
yet we hunger for the "security" of weapons and walls.
You teach us that freedom comes in loving service,
yet we trample on others in our efforts to be "free."
Forgive us, God, when we look to the palace
instead of the stable,
when we heed politicians more than prophets.
Renew us with the spirit of Bethlehem,
That we may be better prepared for your coming.
Amen.

Words of Assurance
Mary bore a Son and named him Jesus
for he would save his people from their sins.
Friends, believe the good news that comes from God.
In Jesus Christ we are forgiven.

Prayers at the Table

42 Blessed are you, Creator God.
You have given us a world
that is an endless marvel of birth and new creation.
Atoms, molecules, and cells beyond count,
each plays its part in a drama
that dwarfs human reason and makes our greatest
inventions seem but feeble shadows.
Yet in each generation we have placed ourselves
on thrones of our own construction;
we have gloried in things of the flesh,
turning money and power into gods.
But you, O Lord, have not abandoned us.
You gave to us a child,
born in an out-of-the-way village,
to be teacher, prophet, and savior.
God of our salvation,
with bread and wine we joyfully
remember your gift of Jesus Christ:
his birth, the cause of great rejoicing,
his death, the cause for deep lament,
his resurrection, the cause for endless wonder,
and his return, the cause for eager hope.
Through this same Jesus Christ we offer
you this prayer. Amen.

43 Leader   Loving God, in this time of waiting we remember
your wondrous acts for our salvation. We remember
how in the beginning you created the heavens and
the earth and made man and woman in your image.
(Genesis 1)

People **My soul waits for the Lord,
and in God's word I hope.**

Leader We remember how you spoke through your prophets
of a child who will be called Wonderful Counselor,
Mighty God, Everlasting Father, Prince of Peace.
(Isaiah 9)

People **My soul waits for the Lord,
and in God's word I hope.**

Leader We remember how you spoke to your chosen one,
Mary, saying "Behold, you will bear a Son whose
Kingdom will have no end." (Luke 1)

People   **My soul waits for the Lord,
and in God's word I hope.**

Leader   We remember the stories of his birth, how the star shone on his manger and the angels proclaimed, "Glory to God in the highest, and peace to God's people on earth." (Luke 2)

People   **My soul waits for the Lord,
and in God's word I hope.**

Leader   We remember how he emptied himself, taking the form of a servant, obedient even to death on a Cross. (Philippians 2)

People   **My soul waits for the Lord,
and in God's word I hope.**

Leader   We remember also his last meal with his closest disciples. How he took bread . . .

44   Leader   In this season of joy and plenty,
People   **We remember those who are sorrowful and in need.**
Leader   In this season of expectation,
People   **We remember those without hope.**
Leader   In this season of the birth of a child,
People   **We pray that all children may know your healing love.**

Leader   God of tenderness and compassion at this table where we break the loaf and drink from the cup,
People   **We remember those who lack daily bread.**
Leader   At this table where we gather in closest fellowship,
People   **We remember those without community.**
Leader   At this table where we remember the gift of God in Jesus Christ,
People   **We pray for the strength to become the body of Christ given for the world.**

45   *For the loaf*
Holy God, your glory lights heaven
and fills the earth with dazzling brightness.
To you the whole creation cries in joy.
We praise you for your Word
by which you made everything that was made,
and which came to shine
in the darkness of our world.
We bring you this bread,

giving thanks for Jesus Christ,
your Word made flesh.
Open our eyes to see the light he brings.
Open our hearts to receive the power he gives.
Open our lives to do the work he assigns.
For in his name we pray. Amen.

46 *For the cup*
Gracious Father, whose Son Jesus Christ
is the eternal Word of power and glory:
we give you thanks for this cup of blessing
with which we remember Jesus,
who lived among us full of grace and truth.
Send your Spirit to this communion feast,
so that as we eat the bread and drink the wine
we may be nourished by Christ's own life,
enlightened by Christ's own light,
and inspired by Christ's own self.
All this we ask in Jesus' name. Amen.

(based on John 1:1-18)

Closing Words

47 May God make us watchful and keep us faithful as we await the coming of Christ our Savior.

48 May our joy be deepened, our faith strengthened, our lives extended that others may see Christ born in our lives.

49 May the child of Bethlehem grant you peace. We go from here to follow his star!

50 Pray in the Holy Spirit; keep yourselves in the love of God; wait for the mercy of our Lord Jesus Christ.

(from Jude 20-21)

Resources for Christmas Day

Greeting

51 Leader Be not afraid; for behold, I bring you good news of a great joy which will come to all people; for to you is born this day in the city of David a Savior, who is Christ the Lord (Luke 2:10-11).

People **For to us a child is born, to us a son is given; and the government will be upon his shoulders, and his name will be called "Wonderful Counselor, Mighty God, Everlasting Father, Prince of Peace"** (Isaiah 9:6).

An alternative form, especially appropriate for this festive occasion, is to mix the spoken biblical narrative with a choral response as the call to worship.

52   Leader   And the angel said to them, "Be not afraid; for behold, I bring you good news of a great joy which will come to all the people; for to you is born this day in the city of David a Savior, who is Christ the Lord" (Luke 2:10-11).

Choir (or congregation) "Angels from the Realms of Glory," first stanza.

Leader   And the shepherds said to one another,"Let us go over to Bethlehem and see this thing that has happened, which the Lord has made known to us" (Luke 2:15).

Choir (or congregation) Second stanza, changing "man" to "us" in the second line.

Leader   And wise men from the East came to Jerusalem, saying, "Where is he who has been born king of the Jews? For we have seen his star in the East, and have come to worship him" (Matthew 2:1-2).

Choir (or congregation) Third stanza

Leader   And Simeon took the child up in his arms and blessed God and said, "Lord, now let your servant depart in peace, according to your word; for my eyes have seen your salvation" (Luke 2:28-30).

Choir (or congregation) Fourth stanza

Opening Prayer
53   God, help us to know your presence and to worship you!
Show us that the star shines before us
if we will but see it,
that the song of great joy is sung for us
if we will but hear it,
that the Prince of Peace is born in our midst
if we will but give him place.
Teach us in this hour to run with the shepherds,
to kneel with the kings,
and to sing your praises with the choir of heaven.
Amen.

Prayers of the People
On this day when so many words are spoken, it is appropriate to

use a bidding prayer to invite quiet, prayerful meditation.

54 On this day when we celebrate the birth of a child, I bid your prayers for all children, especially those in need of a parent's love.

Silence

On this day when we celebrate the Prince of Peace born in our midst, I bid your prayers for the peace of the world, especially for an end to conflict in _____ .

Silence

On this day of presents and feasts, I bid your prayers for the poor and the hungry, especially those in _____ .

Silence

On this day of family and friends, I bid your prayers for the lonely and homeless, especially those in _____ .

Silence

God, you have made the world your cradle and filled it with the most perfect gift. Hear our prayers for the world you have so loved, for we pray in the name of Christ our Savior. Amen.

Invitation to the Lord's Table

55 We come to this table as a people unprepared. Our world is as unready for the coming of Emmanuel as was the crowded town of Bethlehem. We are as unattuned to the eternal as the sleeping shepherds in the field. Our expectations are as unclear as those of the travelers from the East. Though we are unprepared, though our lives are unworthy offerings, God has forgiven our sins and offered us newness of life through Jesus Christ. This is the grace of God in which we participate at this table. Come, share the feast.

Prayer at the Table

56 **People** **Blessed are you, O Lord our God,**
Source of all new life!

Leader You gave to Sarah a child, Isaac,
and renewed with him the covenant.

People **Blessed are you, O Lord our God,**
Source of all new life!

Leader You heard the prayer of Hannah
and gave to her a son, Samuel,
a leader of the people Israel.

People **Blessed are you, O Lord our God,**
Source of all new life!

Leader By your will Elizabeth gave birth
to the prophet, John, who would
prepare the way for our Lord.

People **Blessed are you, O Lord our God,**
Source of all new life!

Leader And when the time had come,
you sent your Spirit upon your servant, Mary,
that she would be the mother of the Christ,
at whose birth new life begins!

People **Blessed are you, O Lord our God,**
Source of all new life!

Pastor We come to this table, blessed God,
to remember this same Jesus Christ.
On the night when he was betrayed . . .

Or this:

57 Pastor Blessed are you, O Lord our God,
Source of all new life!
You gave to Sarah a child, Isaac,
and renewed with him the covenant.
You heard the prayer of Hannah
and gave to her a son, Samuel,
a leader of the people Israel.

People **By your will Elizabeth gave birth**
to the prophet, John, who would
prepare the way for our Lord.
And when the time had come,
you sent your Spirit upon your servant, Mary,
that she would be the mother of the Christ,
at whose birth new life begins!

Pastor We come to this table, God of life,
to remember this same Jesus Christ.
On the night when he was betrayed . . .

Prayer After Communion

58 We thank you, loving God, for Jesus who came long ago as your beloved Child and who has come again in this feast of joy to be our light, our hope, our life. Help us to live in the joy and peace that only Christ can bring. In this name we pray. Amen.

Closing Words

59 May the Spirit of God fill you with the joy, hope, and peace of this season.

THE SEASON AFTER EPIPHANY

Epiphany is both a festive day and a season in the church's annual celebration of Jesus Christ as Word of God and Savior. The word comes from the Greek *epiphaneia* which means appearance, showing forth, or manifestation. The Day of Epiphany is related to Christmas much as Pentecost is related to Easter: it expresses the gradual manifestation of God to the world. There are three "epiphanies" traditionally associated with this season. (1) Through the visit of the Magi to the stable in Bethlehem, the Light is made known to the world. (2) Jesus' baptism in the Jordan before the Jews represents God's manifestation to the chosen people. (3) The miracle at the wedding in Cana in the presence of the disciples is seen as God's epiphany to the church. All three are manifestations of God in the world.

The feast of the Epiphany was the original festival of the incarnation and was celebrated on January 6, a date that had once been the winter solstice in the eastern part of the ancient world. January 6 had long been celebrated by people in the Mediterranean world, and Christians adopted some of its motifs when they identified Jesus with this day. Epiphany was a unitive festival that celebrated both the incarnation and the baptism of Jesus. By the fourth century, Christians in the west had developed a celebration of the birth of Jesus on December 25 which was then the date of the winter solstice in the western regions of the church. In both east and west, the need arose to sort out the several elements that had once been concentrated in festivals on January 6. In the western church, birth narratives and the proclamation of the Incarnation were commemorated on the December date and the visit of the Magi and the baptism of Jesus were left with the January date. In both east and west, the primary symbols growing out of these differing emphases of Epiphany are water, wine, and light.

75

The season extends from January 6, the feast day of the Epiphany, to the Sunday in the liturgical year which marks Jesus' transfiguration on the mountain top (Luke 9:29-30). It is a period lasting from five to nine weeks, ending the day before Ash Wednesday. During this time, in addition to celebrating the journey of the Magi and Jesus' baptism, Christians study the life and ministry of Jesus on earth. The lessons of Epiphany follow Jesus from his baptism by John, to his time in the wilderness, and then to his declaration in the synagogue, "Today this scripture has been fulfilled in your hearing" (Luke 4:21b). They include Jesus' parables, the miracle stories, the beatitudes, and the sermons on the mount and on the plain. It is a time when God's presence is revealed in the midst of human life—through Jesus' ministry and in the church.

Finally, because the Magi are known traditionally as "foreigners from the East"—i.e., those outside the Jewish community—Epiphany is often seen as a time to emphasize global concerns and the mission of the church to the world. But this is a secondary theme to the revealing of Christ—God incarnate—in the world.

Worship Resources for Epiphany

Greetings
60   Leader   And you, O Bethlehem, in the land of Judah are by no means least among the rulers of Judah; for from you shall come a ruler who will govern my people Israel (Micah 5:2).

People   **And lo, the star which they had seen in the East went before them, till it came to rest over the place where the Child was.**

Leader   When they saw the star they rejoiced exceedingly with great joy (Matthew 2:9).

People   **We are here today because we, too, have seen and know the Star. Let us rejoice exceedingly with great joy!**

61   Leader   Arise, shine; for your light has come.
People   **The glory of the Lord has risen upon you.**
Leader   For behold; darkness shall cover the earth
and thick darkness the people.
People   **But the Lord has come;
God's glory is upon us;**

God's light will shine through us
into the world.
Come, let us worship the Light.
Welcome the Son. Praise God.

(adapted from Isaiah 60:1-2)

62 Leader Who are the wise among us?
People **Those who follow the light of truth.**
Leader Why have we come to this place?
People **This is the house of the Lord.
We come to praise God;
to fall down before the Christ;
to offer our humble gifts.**
Leader What gifts do we bring?
People **With the ancient Magi, we come with three gifts:
our heart, and soul, and mind—these three,
which sing with one voice, Alleluia!
Christ is come!**

Opening Prayers
63 Faithful God,
Your love has come into our midst interrupting
the restless wandering of our lives.
Its piercing light leads us, with the ancient Magi,
to the rough-hewn stable and to Jesus,
the infant prince of peace.
And here you call forth from us our gifts:
All our heart
and all our soul
and all our mind.
Holy God, with all our strength
we worship you. Amen.

64 Glorious God, wondrous Light and Spirit,
made known to us by Jesus Christ,
descend upon our hearts.
Pierce with the fire of your presence;
fill with the abundance of your love.
Hold us close with the gentle arm of a parent.
Bring forth from our lips your command,
"The Lord our God is one Lord
There will be no other gods before you."
Amen.

65   God of the wondrous star, Maker of light,
     whose brilliance leads us to
     the manger and back into the night,
     Fill us with your radiance, with the beauty
     that shines in the face of Jesus Christ,
     that we may become signs of your
     Light in all we do and say and are.
     Amen.

Prayers of Confession

66   Mother and Father of us all,
     you have called us to act justly, to love tenderly,
     and to walk humbly before you.
     But we have failed to live as you would have us do,
     and come now to confess our sins:
     unjust acts of commission and omission,
     a refusal to love those who need your tender mercy,
     self-centered lives in which you have no place.
     We are truly sorry, Lord, and ask your forgiveness.
     Open our ears to your voice,
     our lives to your action,
     our hearts and minds to your all-forgiving love.
     Amen.

Words of Assurance

The Light has come that we might believe and be saved. This is the
good news, friends: that Jesus the Christ is in the world, loving us
into the life for which God calls us. Our sins are forgiven by the
one whose power it is to forgive.

67   Leader   Gracious God, Giver of light and life, our lives are
              marked by your presence in the world. But we con-
              fess that we have not followed the path to which we
              are called by the life, death, and resurrection of Jesus
              Christ.
     Right   We have not loved as he loved. We have not minis-
              tered to those around us as he did. We have not
              walked in obedience to your will as he walked.
     Left   We have been blessed by your abundant gifts with-
              out giving to others in return. We have been sup-
              ported by your love without lending support to
              those who need a word of hope. We have lived only

for ourselves, denying life to others by our self-centeredness.

All **For all these sins, dear God, we ask your forgiveness. Give us gentle hearts that we might not add to the world's sorrow. Give us loving hearts that we might share our abundance with the world. Give us courageous hearts that we might walk with Christ— obedient even to death. All this we ask through our Savior, Jesus Christ. Amen.**

Words of Assurance

This is the good news. Christ has come that we might have life and have it abundantly. Children of God, hear these words and believe.

68 A Reading of Scripture for Epiphany
(Isaiah 42:1-9)

Leader Behold my servant, whom I uphold, my chosen, in whom my soul delights. I have put my spirit upon him; he will bring forth justice to the nations. He will not cry or lift up his voice, or make it heard in the street;

People **A bruised reed he will not break, and a dimly burning wick he will not quench; he will faithfully bring forth justice.**

Leader Thus says God, the Lord, who created the heavens and stretched them out, who spread forth the earth and what comes from it, who gives breath to the people upon it and spirit to those who walk in it:

People **"I am the Lord, I have called you in righteousness, I have taken you by the hand and kept you; I have given you as a covenant to the people, a light to the nations, to open the eyes that are blind, to bring out the prisoners from the dungeon, from the prison those who sit in darkness.**

Leader I am the Lord, that is my name; my glory I give to no other, nor my praise to graven images.

People **Behold, the former things have come to pass, and new things I now declare; before they spring forth I tell you of them."**

69 The Beatitudes
Blessed are the poor in spirit,
  for theirs is the kingdom of heaven.
Blessed are those who mourn,
  for they shall be comforted.
Blessed are the meek,
  for they shall inherit the earth.
Blessed are those who hunger and thirst for righteousness,
  for they shall be satisfied.
Blessed are the merciful,
  for they shall see mercy.
Blessed are the pure in heart,
  for they shall see God.
Blessed are the peacemakers,
  for they shall be called children of God.

(from Matthew 5:2-7)

An Offertory Prayer
70 God of majesty and glory, by your Holy Spirit
    make present in us the light that burst
    upon the world when Jesus was born.
    And with that light give us wisdom and courage
    so that in our time we may repair ruined cities
    and proclaim the year of your favor.
    Make us shine like stars in a dark world,
    holding forth the word of life.
    Yours will be the glory and honor.
    Through Jesus Christ we pray. Amen.

Prayers at the Table
71 *For the Bread*
    Generous God, we bring you this loaf
    and remember Jesus.
    He broke bread with friends and strangers,
    turning every meal into an act of praise
    and a covenant of solidarity
    with people everywhere.
    By your Holy Spirit be present here
    as we break bread together.
    May this meal become communion with the living Christ
    and with the people whom Christ loves.
    In this feast of life, give us a foretaste

of the heavenly banquet when we
will break bread with you. Amen.

72 **For the Cup**
Joyful God, we bring this cup,
filled with the fruit of the vine,
and remember Jesus.
At the wedding in Cana, his first miracle,
Jesus turned water into wine
and the people blessed you.
God of life, we pray that your Holy Spirit
will be present in our celebration.
May this wine of the earth be changed
so that we are refreshed with the wine of heaven,
Christ's own blood given for us.
In the name of Jesus we offer you these prayers.
Amen.

73 Leader God of great beauty, we offer you our
thankful praise for giving us creation.
You made the sky, filling it with sun
and moon and stars for us to admire.
You made the earth, filling it with trees
and mountains and animals for us to enjoy.
You made man and woman in your own image,
filling us with dreams and powers to use and
enjoy everything else in your whole creation.
To you be glory and praise.

People **Yet from the beginning we have wasted your gifts,
and the world groans in pain.
Therefore you came to live among us
and in Jesus showed how life should be.
For this greatest gift of all we now praise you.**

Leader With bread and wine and other gifts offered here
to you, we remember his life of mercy and strength,
his teachings on trusting you to care for us,
his death upon the cross for our salvation,
and his rising from the dead to live with you.
For the new life that you offer us through
faith in Jesus Christ, we give you thanks.

People   O God, our whole selves are what we return
penitently and lovingly.
By your Holy Spirit come to us
with the help we need.
Make us what we can be.
Strengthen us every day of our lives
until that time comes when all things
are made perfect by your power.
Through Jesus Christ we pray. Amen.

Benedictions

74   Leader   We came to this place to praise God; to give
thanks for the birth of our Savior, Jesus Christ;
to offer the gifts of heart and soul and mind.

People   **But we cannot linger here, for he is in the world
where we must be—ever singing with one voice,
Alleluia! Christ has come!**

75   Leader   You have seen the Child, offered your gifts,
been changed by the Light.

People   **Now go, bearing the news of his marvelous light
into the world.**

Leader   But beware. The world did not love him,
and persecuted those who did.

People   **And being warned in a dream not to return
to Herod, they departed to their own country,
by another way. Alleluia!
Christ has overcome the world!**

(from Matthew 2:12)

76   Leader   The message of the star—God is in the world.
The message of the Magi—Wisdom follows Truth.
The message of the manger—God's Word comes
where we least expect to find it.

People   **The message for us—Go forth from this place
to bring the Word into the world.**

Leader   We have seen the star and followed it.
We have knelt at the manger and found God.

People   **Christ is in the world!
Thanks be to God! Amen.**

77   Leader   The Lord is with us.
God's presence in the world calls us
to our ministry.

People   **To open the eyes that are blind,
to bring the prisoner from the darkened cell
out into the marvelous light,
to support the bruised reed,
to shelter the dimly burning wick,
to faithfully bring forth God's justice.**

Leader   Go now with the knowledge that all things
are possible for those who wait upon the Lord.

People   **Thanks be to God!**

THE SEASON OF LENT

The season of Lent is a time when the church gathers its energies and directs its life for the great celebration of Easter which is the high point of the Christian year. Lent begins with Ash Wednesday and concludes with the Saturday before Easter. Recalling a symbolic biblical number, this season consists of forty weekdays. Although Sundays are not included within the season itself, Lent does influence the character of these Sundays leading up to Easter. There are four important emphases for Christian worship during this season.

(1) One of the most ancient purposes of Lent is the preparation of candidates for baptism at Easter. For those already baptized, Lent is a time for remembering their baptism and renewing baptismal vows. For everyone, the season affirms that life is generated anew by baptism into Christ. This emphasis upon baptism is especially important in churches which claim believer's baptism as the primary mode of initiation into Christ.

(2) Lent is also a time for the church to meditate upon the meaning of the cross in Christian faith and life. The height and depth of Easter joy is directly proportional to the intensity of our awareness of the cross.

(3) Lent can be a period of increased attention to spiritual discipline, to the fundamental dimensions of life, and to our relationship with God. A common practice is fasting, a significant reduction in eating and drinking for the purposes of self-examination and purification. This Lenten discipline recalls Jesus' self-denial which led to the cross and which makes it possible for us to

yield our whole selves to God. Lenten self-denial gives opportunity for increased study and prayer and also can lead Christians to assume special responsibilities for the sake of the world.

(4) Over the years the confession of sin has had a prominent place in Lent. Candidates for baptism confess their sins; and all Christians are driven to confession when we recognize that we, too, commit the sin that led to the crucifixion of Christ. The mood of Lent is sober and solemn. We approach the cross with a deep awareness of the sacrifice it represents. We also come in confidence that God uses the cross of Christ, and the crosses which we *daily* take up, as instruments for the saving of the world.

These four important dimensions of the meaning of Lent can provide motifs for Lenten worship materials. The elements of the service can weave together themes and images of baptism, the cross, spiritual discipline, and confession, drawing upon scripture, tradition, and contemporary life. Worship leaders could emphasize one of these themes for the entire Lenten season, using it to develop each Sunday's material. They could emphasize a different dimension on each Sunday of the season or mix the emphases over the season.

The first set of materials presented in the following section, consisting of greetings, prayers of confession, and assurances of pardon, is unified by the themes of baptism. The second set is a series of meditations on the cross. These two sets illustrate different ways of developing thematic unity through the Sundays in Lent. The leading accents of the baptismal material are drawn from an ecumenical consensus document which states that baptism is participation in the death and resurrection of Christ, washing, the receiving of the Holy Spirit, incorporation into the body of Christ, and the sign of God's sovereignty in the world (*Baptism, Eucharist and Ministry* [Geneva: World Council of Churches, 1983]). The opening words are printed as a dialogue between leader and people. They could also be read by one person or by two leaders alternating the lines.

Remembering Our Baptism

FIRST SUNDAY OF LENT: Baptism as participation in the death and resurrection of Christ

Opening Words
78   Leader   Through baptism we die and rise with Christ.

People   **God makes the waters of baptism a tomb for the power of sin and death.**

Leader   We are raised from the grave by the glory of God.

People   **Life is made new every day.**

Leader   Because we have been baptized, let us worship God.

(adapted from Romans 6:3-4)

(*An alternate ending*)

Leader   In this hour of worship, let all that we do and sing, all that we pray and preach, all that we touch and taste, be baptized by God's glory.

Prayer of Confession

79   Holy God, in Christ Jesus you promise new life.
Yet we cling to the old life with its broken form
instead of seeking the wholeness of life
which you intend for us.
We glory not in the death of Christ
but in our own achievements.
We build walls that separate us from one another,
and hide behind them.
Today we remember our baptism
and are convicted of our sins.
Forgive us, we pray, in the name of
our Savior Jesus Christ. Amen.

Assurance of Pardon

80   If we have been united with Christ Jesus in a death like his, we shall certainly be united with him in a resurrection like his. In death he died to sin once and for all. In life he lives to God. So we also must consider ourselves dead to sin and alive to God in Christ Jesus.
Friends, believe the good news that comes from God:
In Jesus Christ we are forgiven.

(adapted from Romans 6:5-11)

SECOND SUNDAY OF LENT: Baptism As Washing

Opening Words

81   Leader   When we are baptized, the stain of sin
is washed away.

People   **We are cleansed and made ready
for new life and service.**

Leader   Like clothes from the laundry, ready to be worn,

People **Like a chalkboard wiped and prepared for writing,**
Leader Like hands washed and ready for the table,
People **So we are cleansed by the waters of baptism**
and prepared for the life of love and good works.
Leader Because we have been baptized, let us worship God.

Prayer of Confession
82   O God, in your holy presence we recognize
our uncleanness and confess it to you:
failures to carry out responsibilities,
unwitting alliances with evil,
the bending of moral principles,
the abuse of power,
the pursuit of the lesser goods of life.
In this hour of worship we confess it all to you.
Renew in us the memory of our baptism
when our sins were washed away by
the blood of our Savior Jesus Christ,
in whose name we pray. Amen.

Assurance of Pardon
83   When Christ had offered for all time a single sacrifice for
sins, he sat down at the right hand of God, there to wait until
his enemies should be made a stool for his feet. For by a
single offering he has perfected for all time those who are
sanctified (Hebrews 10:12-14).
Friends, believe the good news that comes from God:
In Jesus Christ we are forgiven.

THIRD SUNDAY OF LENT: Baptism As the Gift of the Holy Spirit

Opening Words
84   Leader   When we are baptized, God gives the gift of the
Holy Spirit.
People **Young men and women shall prophesy.**
Leader The old shall see visions and dream dreams.
People **By the Spirit's power the sick shall be healed,**
evil destroyed, and the works of God made known
in all the earth.
Leader Remembering our baptism in water and the Spirit,
let us worship God.
(based on Joel 3:28-32)

Prayer of Confession
85   Generous God, you have given us
the gift of the Holy Spirit,
but we have refused it.
Not trusting the Spirit's ecstasy,
we crave the pleasures of food, drink, and drugs.
Not content with the joy and vitality that the Spirit gives,
we seek our own inspiration
in self-serving goals of career and social prestige.
Forgive us, we pray, for spurning the gift of the Spirit
and for manipulating others for our own gain.
Forgive us for filling the emptiness of life with noise
instead of letting your Spirit make us silent
in the face of your mystery and glory.
We pray in the name of Jesus, our Savior. Amen.

Assurance of Pardon
86   Repent and be baptized every one of you in the name of Jesus
Christ for the forgiveness of your sins and you shall receive
the gift of the Holy Spirit.
Friends, believe the good news that comes from God:
In Jesus Christ we are forgiven.

FOURTH SUNDAY OF LENT: Baptism As Incorporation
Into the Body of Christ

Opening Words
87   Leader   The waters of baptism are the waters
                 of the womb of God.
     **People   When we are baptized, we are born
                 into a new family.**
     Leader   There is neither Jew nor Greek, slave nor free,
                 male nor female.
     **People   We are united with all who confess Christ
                 in Manila and Moscow, in Rome and Rio.**
     Leader   We lift our different voices as one body,
                 in praise of the one God, who gives birth
                 to this new family by baptism into Christ.
                                          (based on Galatians 3:26-29)

Prayer of Confession

88 O God, you seek to make one great human family,
but we break it into factions
and fight among ourselves.
You have created us to be equal in your sight,
molded and restrained by your law,
and freed by faith in Christ from slavery to sin.
Yet we separate into black and white, management and labor,
communist and capitalist, rich and poor,
each group arrayed against the others.
We confess these sins against you and against
the family born from the womb of your love.
Forgive us and restore unity to your broken world.
In the name of Jesus Christ we pray. Amen.

Assurance of Pardon

89 Everyone who is in Christ has become a new creation. The old is gone and the new has come. God, through Christ, has reconciled the world and gives us the ministry of reconciliation (based on 2 Corinthians 5:17-18).
Friends, believe the Good News that comes from God:
In Jesus Christ we are forgiven.

FIFTH SUNDAY OF LENT: Baptism As Sign of God's Holy Commonwealth

Opening Words

90 Leader With the cross God claims the world!
People **and with the resurrection shows that love is the power in all of life.**
Leader By baptism God makes us to be signs of love's renewing power,
People **and calls us to live in trust and helpfulness.**
Leader In our worship today let us yield ourselves again to God's sovereignty.
People **And pray for power to be obedient and bold.**

Prayer of Confession

91 O God, in Jesus Christ you revealed
your holy commonwealth to be a rule of love.
But the people long ago crucified him,
and we crucify him still.

We turn from your love,
seeking security in wealth and weapons.
At the expense of others we build little empires
to please our egos, but are never satisfied.
We turn away from your justice
to bribery, manipulation, extortion, and murder.
Remembering our baptism, when we confessed
that Jesus Christ is lord, we come to you,
asking forgiveness. Amen.

Assurance of Pardon
92   Once you were separated from Christ, alienated from the commonwealth of Israel and strangers to the covenants of promise, with no hope and without God in the world. But now in Christ Jesus, you who once were far off have been brought near in the blood of Christ. For he is our peace, who has made us both one, and has broken down the dividing wall of hostility (Ephesians 2:12-15).
Friends, believe the good news that comes from God:
In Jesus Christ we are forgiven.

Meditations on the Cross

While the cross is always the central symbol of the Christian life, it is given special attention during Lent. These meditations provide ways by which congregations can focus week by week on the cross. All use Galatians 6:14, and are based on passages from Hans-Ruedi Weber's *On a Friday Noon*. The hymn verses at the beginning and ending of each meditation may be said or sung.

These meditations can be used in the Sunday service as affirmations of faith, as part of the prayers of the people, or as part of the devotions at the Lord's table. Silence before and after the meditations may enhance their contribution to the service. The life and tradition of the church are filled with art that can be adapted for Lenten worship. For example, slides of paintings of the crucifixion could provide a visual context for praying these meditations on the cross.

93   Cantor   "When I survey the wondrous cross
On which the Prince of glory died,
My richest gain I count but loss,
And pour contempt on all my pride."

Leader   God be praised for the wondrous cross,
         the tree of life,
Left   Which bears upon itself the scars
         and wounds of the world,
Right   Yet heals the sick, brings hope to the
         desperate, and comforts the oppressed.
Left   God be praised for the cross
         which guides the lost, feeds the hungry,
         and shelters the poor;
Right   Inspires the anxious, illumines the wise,
         and challenges the fearless;
Unison   Saves the condemned, and meets the need
         of every age and every land.
Leader   God forbid that we should glory,
         except in the cross of Jesus Christ our Lord.
Unison   "When I survey the wondrous cross
         On which the Prince of glory died,
         My richest gain I count but loss,
         And pour contempt on all my pride."

(Inspired by a sermon of John Mbiti, Uganda, 1972)

94 Cantor "When I survey the wondrous cross
         On which the Prince of glory died,
         My richest gain I count but loss,
         And pour contempt on all my pride."
Women Jesus stretched out his hands during the Passion,
Men   suffering to save those who trusted in him.
Unison He was delivered to destroy death,
         to sever the bonds of Satan,
         destroy hell, lead out the saints,
         and announce his glorious resurrection.
Leader May God be blessed.
Unison and may we find life through the power
         of the cross of Christ.
Leader God forbid that we should glory,
         except in the cross of Jesus Christ our Lord.
Unison "In the cross of Christ I glory,
         Towering o'er the wrecks of time.
         All the light of sacred story
         Gathers round its head sublime."

(Inspired by the Ethiopian Orthodox liturgy)

95   Cantor   "When I survey the wondrous cross
On which the Prince of glory died,
My richest gain I count but loss,
And pour contempt on all my pride."

Choir   Take the good and cast the evil;
Listen, people, to my song.
For 'tis God for whom I'm speaking
To the valiant and the strong.

People   'Tis our sins that have delayed us;
Let us cast them and be free.
Leaving everything behind us,
Finding paradise with thee.

Choir   Take the cross, the cross he died on,
Oh, repay him as you may.
For by dying he redeemed us,
Can we give him less today?

Leader   God forbid that we should glory,
except in the cross of Jesus Christ our Lord.

Unison   "In the cross of Christ I glory,
Towering o'er the wrecks of time.
All the light of sacred story
Gathers round its head sublime."

(Taken from the Chronicles of Normandy, 1145)

96   Cantor   "When I survey the wondrous cross
On which the Prince of glory died,
My richest gain I count but loss,
And pour contempt on all my pride."

Unison   For the cross is the sign of mercy,
the proof of forgiveness,
the vehicle of grace,
and the banner of peace.

Men   The cross breaks down our pride and shatters
our envy.

Women   It redeems our sin and atones for our punishment.

Leader   The cross of Christ is the door to heaven,
the key to paradise, the downfall of the devil,
the uplifting of humankind.

Men   In the cross, God again proved faithful
to the hope of the patriarchs,

the promise of the prophets,
and the ministry of the priests.

Women Tyrants are convicted by the cross
and the mighty defeated.
It lifts up the miserable and honors the poor.

Unison The cross is the end of darkness,
the spreading of light, the flight of death.

Leader God forbid that we should glory,
except in the cross of Jesus Christ our Lord.

Unison "In the cross of Christ I glory,
Towering o'er the wrecks of time.
All the light of sacred story
Gathers round its head sublime."

(Adapted from Rupert, Abbot of Duetz, 12th century)

97 Cantor "When I survey the wondrous cross
On which the Prince of glory died,
My richest gain I count but loss,
And pour contempt on all my pride."

Unison The mystery of the cross shines out in glory,
the cross on which Life suffered death
and by that death gave back life to us.

Leader God has reigned from a tree.

Unison Hail, cross, our only hope!
In this season of the Passion,
give an increase of grace to the good,
and wipe out the sins of the guilty.

Leader Let every spirit praise you,
fount of salvation, Holy Trinity.

Unison On those to whom you have generously given
the victory of the cross,
bestow the reward also!

Leader God forbid that we should glory,
except in the cross of Jesus Christ our Lord.

Unison "In the cross of Christ I glory,
Towering o'er the wrecks of time.
All the light of sacred story
Gathers round its head sublime."

(Inspired by the passion hymn of
Venatius Fortunatus, 6th century)

Worship Resources for Lent

Affirmations of Faith

Passages of scripture which focus on redemption through suffering are especially appropriate as affirmations of faith during Lent. One such passage is Isaiah 53:1-5 from which the following is adapted.

98 Leader Who has believed what we have heard?
People **To whom has the arm of God been revealed?**
Leader Holy Jesus, suffering servant, we remember you.
People **Growing up like a tender plant and**
like a root out of dry ground
you had no beauty or comeliness,
but were despised, rejected,
and acquainted with grief.
You carried our sorrows,
were wounded for our transgressions,
and bruised for our iniquities.
You suffered the punishment
that makes us whole
and the stripes by which we are healed.
Leader Jesus, Savior, we honor you.

99 God is a God of infinite Goodness,
who does not will death but life in all its fullness,
who treasures the poor, the lost drachma,
the stray sheep, the prodigal.
Captured at night, taken away by soldiers,
stripped of his garments, interrogated, tortured,
crowned with sharp thorns
and finally condemned to death on a cross,
Jesus entered into solidarity
with all the downtrodden of history.
But three days after his death,
Jesus emerged alive.
Death has been swallowed up in Christ's resurrection.
Oppression has been transformed into a pathway

of liberation through sacrifice.
We are destined and called to live to the full:
joyous in our hope, confident in our love,
and reconciled to the world,
our fellow human beings, and God.
Alleluia. Amen.

Invitations to the Table

It is especially appropriate that during Lent and the Sundays in this period the Invitations to the table focus on the cross as the means of redemption. Even the other Lenten themes of baptism, spiritual discipline, and confession find their source and destination in the cross and resurrection. Further, the self-giving of Christ makes possible the self-giving of Christians for God, for one another, and for the world.

100 We come to the table, cast in the shadow of two trees.
The first is rough-hewn into a cross,
stripped of bark and leaves,
planted into the ground
with human life nailed to its outstretched arms.
This barren tree, with Jesus' blood upon it,
becomes fruitful in the second tree,
the leaves of which are for the healing of the nations.
It blossoms in the new Jerusalem
and signals the coming of peace to all creation.
Come to the table.
Bring the gifts of the earth.
Rest in the shade of the tree.
Receive the gifts of healing and life.

101 In this season of the church's year, we are drawn to high drama. We set the table with money gained from our work, offerings freely given as symbols of our lives. And this table, prepared by our gifts of coin and cup, shows forth the full character of the drama. In broken bread we see, sense, and symbolize the sacrifice made once and for all. In poured out wine, we reconsider, recall, and remember the offering Jesus made for us. We become actors on this stage, coming into full identity as we give and receive. All who are baptized into Jesus Christ are invited to participate. Come, step into the reality of God's drama.

Prayers at the Table

The Lenten prayers at the Lord's table can draw upon images of the redemptive suffering of Jesus as reason for thankful praise. Because the path which led to the cross ends at the resurrection, the prayers also need to point to the living presence of Christ which continues to redeem even the time being.

The following prayer is developed around the theme of the cross of Christ becoming the tree of life.

102 Pastor   Holy God, we offer you our grateful praise
for the cross of Christ.
In the beginning you created the world,
breathed into us the breath of life,
and gave us a home in Eden,
shaded by the tree of life.

People   **When we ate of the forbidden fruit,
the world fell under the curse,
and we lived east of Eden in sin and suffering.**

Pastor   Yet you stayed with us
in our wanderings through bondage
to deliverance, and from exile to restoration.

People   **You came to us in the suffering servant
whom we reviled, betrayed, and killed.
He bore our sins in his body on the tree
so that we could die to sin and live
to righteousness.**

Pastor   We thank you for taking this cross,
symbol of defiance and death,
and by your resurrecting power,
making it for us the tree of life.

People   **As we eat and drink this bread and wine,
the fruit of this life-giving tree,
we pray that its leaves
will be for the healing of the nations.
And we pray that our cursed world
will become once again a garden like Eden.**

Philippians 2:7-11, a significant Christological hymn of the early church, is the basis of the following prayer.

103 Pastor   Lord Jesus Christ, with this loaf and cup
we offer you our thankful praise.

You were in the form of God
but did not count equality with God
a thing to be grasped.

People **Instead, you emptied yourself,**
took the form of a servant,
and were born in human likeness.
You humbled yourself
and became obedient to death on the cross.

Pastor   We give you thanks, blessed Savior,
that God has highly exalted you,
and given to you the name
that is above every name,
in heaven and on earth and under the earth.
As we eat and drink this bread and wine,
signs of your body and blood given for us,
unite us with yourself in the glory
of your Father's heavenly splendor.

People **And with your people everywhere**
we confess to the glory of God
that you are Lord and Savior.

The following prayers of thanksgiving follow the traditional Disciples pattern of prayers by elders for the bread and the cup. Both prayers pick up the language of Lent and both call upon the Holy Spirit.

104 *Prayer for the Bread*
God of suffering love, we offer you
our thanksgiving for the cross of Christ.
Wood from the forest, alive and green,
was cut down to make a tree of death.
Jesus, cut down in his strength,
was nailed to this cross and died.
With creating power,
you transformed the cross into the tree of life.
Now may your Holy Spirit take this wheat,
cut down, crushed, baked into bread,
and make it for us the source of life.
As we eat of it,
may we receive Christ's body given for us.
May we who are cut down be caused to grow again,
and may our lives blossom with faith and hope. Amen

105 *Prayer for the Cup*

God of our salvation,
when the cross was set in the ground,
with Jesus nailed upon it,
it became for us the tree
which bears the fruit of the resurrection.
As your Holy Spirit moves
in this fruit of the vine,
may it nourish us with the blood of Christ.
As we drink from this cup,
fill us with the power of the resurrection.
Strengthen us to turn away
from trees bearing sickness, suffering, and death.
Refresh us always from this tree
whose fruit is love, joy, peace, and life.
Through our Savior Jesus Christ. Amen.

THE SEASON OF EASTER

Easter is to the church what the deliverance from Egyptian bondage is to the Jewish community: the fundamental revelation of the presence, purpose, and power of God in the world. Out of despair and death on the cross, God brings life. As Christians celebrate this festival of redemption, we experience again the transforming power of God who creates new life among us. We are reminded that God who raised Jesus from the dead can bring life to any situation of death—personal, political, cosmic.

Thus the worship of Easter Day is organized around the generating image of God's causing life to come from death. The Sundays during the season following Easter focus on God's life-giving power in the world. The gospel readings depict the nature and work of the risen Christ. The season is concluded on the Day of Pentecost when the Holy Spirit comes to empower the church to continue this witness to God's power over sin and death.

During this season the arts used in worship are especially important. The world is full of the images of death; in its worship the church can offer images of the life-giving power of God who overcomes the fear of death and stirs people to live in hope and joy. The use of vocal and instrumental music can be expanded so that small singing groups, orchestral ensembles, folk instruments, hand bells, and piano and organ help the people express their joy in Christ. The Easter season is a time to try liturgical drama, mime, and dance; readings of poetry; painting, sculpture, textile art; light shows. During the offertory, members of the congregation could bring to the communion table signs of new life as they experience it. Services could include poetry and hymns written by church members. This is a time for exhibits of art, including posters and drawings by the people.

Services for Easter Day

Paschal Vigil

Many Christians begin their celebration of Easter with the Paschal Vigil on Saturday night, Easter Eve. The name of this service comes from the Latin word *pasche*, which means suffering or passion, and points to the unity of cross and resurrection as one saving event.

Through reading, singing, drama, and prayer, the vigil traces the history of salvation from creation and the fall, through the history of Israel. It comes to a high point in the life, death, and resurrection of Jesus. The order of worship includes a service of baptism and the renewal of baptismal vows, and reaches its climax with the vision of the new heaven and the new earth. The service is timed so that the epic cry, "He is risen!" comes just after midnight, the beginning of Easter Day. Then comes the first celebration of the Easter eucharist. A joyful "breakfast" may follow, especially if members of the church have fasted during these last days of Holy Week.

Easter Sunrise

The sunrise service derives its inspiration from the biblical account of the women discovering the empty tomb very early in the morning. Leaving our homes in the misty pre-dawn darkness, we sense the shadow and mystery with which the resurrection day began. On this Day of Days, the act of coming to a service in the early morning places the worship and praise of God before anything else that we do.

There is no reason for this early service to duplicate the main Sunday service. When celebrated outside, the service may include elements that are made possible by that setting, such as bonfires, processions, and pageants. Often the sunrise service is followed by a congregational breakfast which becomes an extension of worship not unlike the love feasts of early Christian communities.

The Major Easter Service

The major service for Easter Day is a strong testimony to the power of God who overcomes death with life. Because the day is so important for the church calendar, it calls for music, prayers, and celebrations that are strong, beautiful, and more expansive than on ordinary Sundays of the year. Therefore the service must be planned carefully so that the exuberance does not become too much for the people to bear. The Easter sermon may be briefer than usual and its focus should be a testimony to the life-giving power of God.

The Easter service is a time for baptism. As women and men are baptized, they re-enact the drama of Christ's saving actions: death, burial, resurrection, and continuing presence. Candidates are buried in the watery grave and then raised to a new beginning of life. The congregation renews its baptismal vows, thus affirming the desire that its life continue to be formed by the resurrection and enlivened by the risen Christ.

Worship Resources for Easter Day

Greetings

106 Leader My strength, my song is the Lord
who has become my Savior.

People **Glad songs of victory sound
within the tents of the just.**

Leader The Lord works with force,
right hand raised high.

People **I shall not die, but I shall live
to tell the Lord's great deeds.**

(Psalm 118:14-17, ICEL)

107 Leader The tomb is empty.

People **Sound the trumpet.**

[*One trumpet plays measures one and two of
"Christ the Lord Is Risen Today."*]

Leader The Lord is risen!

People **Sound the trumpets!**

[*Two trumpets play measures five and six.*]

Leader Christ leads us on the road to life!

People **Sound the trumpets!**

[*Trumpets and organ play the Alleluia of the hymn
as an introduction for the congregation to sing.*]

Opening Prayers

108 God of life,
the women came to the tomb
on the first day of the week,
hands laden with the spices of sadness.
So we come this morning,
hearts broken by the sin of the world.

You met them in resurrection power
and sent them running down the path
to tell the others
that the tomb was empty.
Meet us this morning
in our songs and story,
in scripture and sacrament.
Reveal to us the risen Christ
so that we too may
tell the good news that
life is stronger than death. Amen.

109 Risen Christ,
as the disciples walked the road of sorrow,
you appeared to them.
Unrecognized, you caused their hearts to burn.
So in this hour of worship,
appear to us as your burning presence:
in the opening of the scriptures,
in the offering of praise, prayer, and petition,
and in the breaking of the bread. Amen.

Affirmations of Faith
110 Lord Jesus Christ,
you are the image of the invisible God,
the first-born of all creation.
In you all things in heaven and earth
were created,
things visible and invisible,
thrones, dominions, principalities, authorities.
You existed before anything else,
and you hold everything together.
You are the head of the body, the church,
the first-born from the dead,
in everything pre-eminent.
In you the fullness of God
was pleased to dwell,
and through you God reconciled
all things on earth and in heaven,
making peace by the blood of the cross.
                        (adapted from Colossians 1:15-20)

111 Left   We have complete confidence in the gospel: It is God's power to save all who believe. Do you believe this?

Right   Yes! God puts us right through faith in Jesus Christ. This is the free gift of God's grace! Do you believe this?

Left   Yes! Because of our sins, Jesus was given over to die; and he was raised to life in order to put us right with God.

Right   So we give ourselves to God as those who have been brought from death to life!

All   The wages of sin is death, but God's free gift is eternal life. Thanks be to God! (based on Paul's affirmations in Rom. 1:16; 3:22-24; 4:25; 6:13, 23, TEV.)

Invitations to the Table

112 At the close of the first resurrection day, Jesus was at table with two disciples with whom he had walked unrecognized on the road. He took bread, blessed and broke it, and gave it to them. Their eyes were opened and they recognized that it was Jesus. In the breaking of bread at this table, this same Jesus is made known to us. Come, eat, that our eyes may be opened, that our hearts may burn within, that Christ may be made know to us.

113 Leader   In the upper room is an empty table.
People   Where have they gone?
Leader   On the lonely hill is an empty cross.
People   Where have they laid the body?
Leader   In the garden is an empty tomb.
People   Where have they taken the Lord?
Leader   On the path a Presence shines.
People   Who can it be?
Leader   In an upper room they lock the door.
People   But Jesus stands within.
Leader   This church becomes an upper room.
People   In its center the table is full.
Leader   Through bread and wine Jesus comes to be with us.
People   Come, let us commune with him.

Prayer at the Table

114 Minister   Holy God, from the beginning of creation
you have demonstrated your will
to bring life out of death.

People   **Alleluia!**

Single Voices

One   When the fierce, primeval sea
raged against your ordered world,
you made the waters to be
the source of fertility and life.

Two   When Abraham raised the knife
to sacrifice his only son,
you trapped a ram in the thicket
to be the sacrifice and to save the boy.

Three   When the people of Israel
were threatened by the angel of death,
you commanded them to paint their doorposts
with the blood of the lamb,
and their children did not die.

Four   When the valley was filled with dry bones,
you sent the prophet to speak your word.
Sinews came upon the bones,
covering them with flesh,
and they stood on their feet and lived.

Five   When the women came to the tomb
prepared to anoint the body
and abandon all hope,
you rolled away the stone
and revealed the Lord Jesus
risen from the dead.

People   **Holy God, Glory to you!**
Alleluia!

Minister   We give thanks to you, God our Savior,
that you transform death into life,

People   **And that the body and blood of Jesus,**
put to death upon the cross,
becomes the means of life for us.

Minister   We praise you, Holy God,
that over this bread and wine
your Holy Spirit speaks again
the transforming words of Jesus:
This is my body. This is my blood.

People	Release your life-giving power as we partake of the loaf and cup.
Minister	May we who live in the valley of the shadow of death be raised to renewed life and witness.
People	Inspire us to work for that day when Christ shall come again and the whole world shall be raised to glory. Through the same Jesus Christ, with you and the Holy Spirit, one God now and forever. Amen.

Prayers After Communion

115 God of unending life,
as you raised Jesus from the dead,
so with this bread and wine,
you raise us from death
and fill us with your life.
Now reveal your transforming power through us:
in the face of chaos,
in the house where the angel of death stalks,
in each valley of dry bones,
where every tomb is sealed and all hope ended.
Great and living God, may your life shine through us
and all the world become an Alleluia sung to you. Amen.

116 Women Liberating God,
from death you brought Jesus into new life.
Men   From bondage to sin, you bring us to abundant life.
All   Now from this feast of bread and wine
raise us up to speak your name in power
and to live your way in peace. Amen.

Closing Words

117 When the women had seen the empty tomb,
the angel said to them, "Go. Go and tell."
Now that we have seen the empty tomb,
I say to you, "Go. Go and tell."
The Lord is risen.
The Lord is risen indeed.

Worship Resources for the Season of Easter

Greetings

Greetings 118 and 119, each based on a passage of scripture, adapt the original for use in worship by changing it from a statement about God to a prayer offered to God.

118 Leader   With joy and gladness let us honor God.
  People   Holy God, with heart and mind,
  soul and strength, we worship you.
  Leader   For by your great mercy we have been born anew
  into a living hope by the resurrection
  of Jesus Christ from the dead.
  People   Holy God, with joy and gladness
  we honor you.

(based on 1 Peter 1:3-4)

119 Leader   Let us worship God who is rich in mercy.
  People   Because of your great love,
  you brought us to life in Christ
  even when we were dead in our sins.
  Leader   By your grace we are saved,
  through trusting Jesus Christ.
  People   Gracious God, we honor you.

(based on Ephesians 2:4-5)

120 Leader   The night is far spent.
  People   The day is at hand.
  Leader   Come, all who live in darkness.
  People   Christ Jesus is risen from the dead,
  the dawn of God's new day.
  Leader   Come, all whose future is despair.
  People   Christ Jesus is risen from the dead,
  the opening of the door to the future.
  Leader   Come, all whose life is death.
  People   Christ Jesus is risen from the dead,
  the birth of our new life in God.

The following item can be used as an ascription of praise at the beginning of a service or as a response to the Word of God. The leader says each line in a brisk cadence and the congregation repeats in similar fashion. Because the lines are short and their mood is one of free response to God, they do not need to be printed for the congregation.

121 Praise God.
  Christ lives.
  Praise God.
  We live.
  Praise God.
  Death dies.
  Praise God.
  Hope soars.
  Peace comes.
  Love grows.
  Join hands.
  Live now
  with power
  in Christ.
  Lift hands
  to God.
  Christ lives.
  Praise God.
  We live.
  Praise God.

Opening Prayers
122 Blessed God,
  by your great mercy
  we have been born anew.
  In this hour of worship
  stir again the living hope
  which you have given the world
  through the resurrection of Jesus,
  in whose name we pray. Amen.

123 Living God,
  for forty days the risen Christ
  appeared to the disciples long ago:
  on the lonely trail,
  in the quiet upper room,
  by the shore in early morning.
  By your Holy Spirit
  may Christ now appear to us:

on the wings of praise,
in life-giving Word,
in broken bread and poured out wine.
Amen.

Affirmations of Faith

124 Leader   Possessed by the spirit of faith,
             let us declare what we believe.
     **People   God who raised the Lord Jesus to life
             will with Jesus raise us too,
             and will bring us into God's holy presence.**
     Leader   May our chorus of thanksgiving ascend
             to the glory of God.

> (adapted from 2 Corinthians 4:13-15)

125 Leader   Jesus said, "If you believe in me,
             even though you die, yet you shall live."
             Do you believe this?
     **People   Yes, we believe that Jesus is the Christ,
             the resurrection and the life,
             who even now is coming into the world.**

> (based on John 11:25-27)

126 Leader   Great indeed, we confess,
             is the mystery of our religion.
     **People   Christ was manifested in the flesh,
             vindicated in the spirit,
             seen by angels,
             preached among the nations,
             believed on in the world,
             taken up in glory.**

> (1 Timothy 3:16)

Invitations to the Table

127 A Dialogue of Jesus with the Disciples
     Leader   Jesus declares: "Do not work for the food which
             cannot last, but work for food that endures to eter-
             nal life."
     **People   The disciples ask, "What must we do if we are to do
             the work God wants?"**
     Leader   "This is working for God, that you believe in the
             one whom God has sent."

People "Then what is the sign that we may see and believe?"

Leader "The bread of God, which comes down from heaven and gives life to the world, that is the sign."

People "Lord, give us this bread always."

Leader Jesus declares, "I am the bread of life. Anyone who comes to me shall not hunger, and anyone who believes in me shall never thirst."

(adapted from John 6:27-35)

128 We come to this table to remember Jesus Christ. He lived among us full of grace and truth. He was made perfect in suffering and has become the pioneer of our salvation. Let us therefore call out our praises and set the table with our thank offerings.

Prayers at the Table

129 Pastor God of majesty,
before the day when you made
the earth and the heavens,
your glory was from everlasting to everlasting.
In thunder, fire, and smoke
you came down in glory on Sinai
and carved your law into tablets of stone.
Sitting on a throne high and lifted up,
you filled the earth with your glory
and through the prophets
proclaimed justice and peace.

People **This same glory we behold in Jesus Christ,
who calmed the stormy sea,
opened the unseeing eyes of the poor,
united your divided family,
destroyed the fear of death,
and now lives with you in the glory of heaven.
God of majesty, all thanks to you!
Now may your glory shine in us.**

Pastor As we receive this holy meal,
fill us with the radiance of Christ's risen life.
Carve your commandments
into the tablets of our hearts.
Cause our tongues to burn
and our voices to cry for justice.

Open our unseeing eyes and stopped up ears.
Bind us together as your one servant people.

People **At last, bring us into the full presence**
of your unfading splendor,
where the multitude of the heavenly
hosts ever cry out,
"Blessing, dominion, honor, and glory!"
Through the same Jesus Christ,
with you and the Holy Spirit,
one God now and forever. Amen.

130 *For the Bread*

Blessed God,
you give us the earth,
rich and fertile.
We plant the seed,
and the earth, nourished by your sun and rain,
brings forth wheat.
Now we bring you this grain
made into bread for the table.
With your Holy Spirit bless this loaf
that we may receive our Savior Jesus Christ
who gave his body as the bread of life.
As we eat at this table,
plant in us spiritual seed
which will grow and mature
into love for you and one another
until that day when we break bread
with you at your heavenly table. Amen

131 *For the Cup*

Generous God,
you plant the earth with choice vines
and bring an abundant harvest of good fruit.
We bring you this cup,
filled with the fruit of the vine,
and offer it to you in thanksgiving
for all that you give us.
Bless this cup with your living Spirit
that we may be joined with Jesus Christ
who shed his blood for the sins of the world.
May this fruit of the vine,

enliven us so that we will become
joyful signs of your life in the world.
Through Jesus Christ we pray. Amen.

132 Leader Holy God, we come to this meal of communion,
     People **asking your forgiveness**
            and offering you our praise.
     Leader O God, help us to remember:
     People **our Savior Jesus, delivered to death**
            for our sins, and raised to life
            that we might be forgiven.
     Leader Inspire us to believe the good news:
     People **that by faith we are made right with you**
            and can live in peace with our Savior.
     Leader Help us to accept the new life:
     People **the life that Jesus gives**
            with grace and goodness.
     Leader Teach us what Jesus expects:
     People **lives of justice, mercy, and good faith.**
     Leader Empower us to act upon the words of Christ:
     People **to be my followers, leave self behind,**
            take up your cross, and come with me.
     Leader Holy God, with loaf and cup, by word and Spirit
            made to be our Savior's body and blood,
     People **we offer you this prayer of petition and praise.**
            Amen.

Prayers After Communion

133 Mighty God, after the risen Lord
had broken bread with those he loved,
he sent them into the world to feed your sheep.
Grant that we may now feed your people
as we live in justice,
remember the poor and dispossessed,
and yield ourselves to you and to one another
in self-giving love.

134 Holy God, when the risen Jesus
met the twelve on the mountaintop,
he commissioned them to baptize and teach.
Now that he has come to us in bread and wine,
symbols of his presence with us,

send us forth to baptize into your company
those who have never known you
and to teach them your ways
of love, power, and justice.

Closing Words

135 Great God of peace,
you brought again from the dead
our Lord Jesus Christ,
the great shepherd of the sheep.
By the blood of the eternal covenant,
equip us with everything good,
that we may do your will,
working through us,
all that is pleasing in your sight.
Through the same Jesus Christ,
to whom be glory for ever and ever. Amen.
(adapted from Hebrews 13:20-21)

136 Sisters and brothers,
you have died to sin.
Now you belong to the One
who has been raised from the dead
so that you may bear fruit for God.
(adapted from Romans 7:4)

THE SEASON AFTER PENTECOST

Pentecost is the longest season of the Christian year, lasting about six months. During the first half of the year, from Advent through Pentecost Day, the church re-enacts the drama of redemption through Jesus Christ, God with us in human form. During the second half of the year, the season of Pentecost, Christians dramatize the continuing redemptive presence of God in the world through the Holy Spirit. We also celebrate the mission of the church as it lives in the world under the power of the Spirit.

Drama of Redemption	Season of the Christian Year
Incarnation	Advent Christmas
Manifestation	Epiphany
Passion	Lent
Resurrection Ascension	Easter
Coming of the Spirit	Pentecost Day
The Church Waits and Witnesses	Season of Pentecost
Coming in Glory	Advent

Several themes run like deep, quiet undercurrents through the Sundays of Pentecost. These include the expansion of the church, growth in the life of discipleship, the mission of the church in the world, and the universality of the church. Among the days of special emphasis are Pentecost Day itself, Trinity Sunday, World

113

Communion Sunday, All Saints Day, Thanksgiving Sunday, and Christ the Cosmic Ruler.

Several considerations suggest that the fall of the year should also include an emphasis upon the creation. Since the Christian year is organized around the drama of redemption, the doctrine of creation receives relatively little attention. The population of North America is becoming increasingly urban, removed from the land and ecologically wasteful. At the same time, the burgeoning world population and the exhaustion of arable land and other natural resources increase the importance of our stewardship of the earth. A season celebrating creation is also a reminder that redemption takes place within the created world that is itself groaning in travail. Coming at the climax of the growing season, an emphasis on creation offers a natural occasion, not only to give thanks for the abundance and goodness of the environment but to remember that the covenant between God and humankind includes the land.

In the Common Lectionary (see pp. 172-191), the first and third readings for each Sunday in Pentecost assume a different relationship to one another than they have in the rest of the Christian year. From Advent through Pentecost Day, the reading from the Hebrew Scriptures provides a thematic accent to the gospel reading. In a significant portion of the Pentecost season, however, this relationship is set aside with favor given to sequential and representative readings from major segments of the Bible of Judaism.

Cycle A: Readings from the first five books
Cycle B: Readings from the stories of David and the Wisdom
　　　　　literature
Cycle C: Readings from the Prophets

Because the Sundays of this season are loosely structured, they provide the occasion for drawing upon topics and themes for preaching and worship which may not arise during the first half of the Christian year. For example, Pentecost provides the opportunity for a series of sermons on a book of the Bible or for a series that interprets social conditions in the light of the gospel.

Pentecost Sunday

The Day of Pentecost celebrates the outpouring of the Holy Spirit on the church. The Spirit, who is the immediate agent of the presence, purpose, and power of God in the world, works in several ways. The Holy Spirit deepens the self and the community into silence; the Spirit also brings about overpowering ecstasy and stimulates many stages of experience between these two extremes. The test of the authenticity of the Spirit is the degree to which it creates a life of enduring discipleship and a community which gathers together people of different races, cultures, classes, and genders, people who have been alienated from one another as at Babel (Genesis 11).

Since a fundamental dimension of the Spirit is power, a major purpose of worship on Pentecost is to portray that power liturgically so that the congregation can experience it. The Holy Spirit is difficult to represent in services of worship. On the first Christian Pentecost (the holiday itself began long before in Judaism), wind and fire were the signs of the Spirit's presence and transformative power. Today, dance, music, and expressive speech take their place in portraying the immediacy and the energy of this divine presence. In the biblical tradition and in much of the church's history, including the meeting at Cane Ridge, the Spirit breaks out in the midst of the congregation in more demonstrable ways—in ways that today are described by the term charismatic.

Since the Jewish Pentecost was a harvest festival, it is appropriate that the congregation rejoice in being harvested by the Spirit of God. In many places fruit, berries, and early garden produce are already being enjoyed and could provide the substance for a Pentecost festival meal.

Greetings
137 Leader   If God should take back the Spirit
and suck up the life-giving breath,
all flesh would perish and return to dust.

People   **But God says, "I will pour out my Spirit.
I will pour out my Spirit on all flesh."**

(from Job 34:14-15; Joel 2:38)

Opening Prayer
138 Holy Spirit of God,
Come as the fire and burn.
Come as the wind and cleanse.
Come as light and reveal.
Convict, convert, consecrate,
until we are wholly yours. Amen.

Litany

The music of the church is filled with songs of the Spirit. In this litany, which could be used as part of the response to the Word of God, a familiar song is used as the congregational response.

139 Choir [*singing*]   Spirit of the living God,
                           Fall afresh on us.

Leader   Spirit of God, when the children of Israel
                           had crossed the Red Sea, you fell upon
                           Miriam and she took timbrel in hand and
                           danced before you.

People [*singing*]   **Spirit of the living God,**
                           Let us dance today.

Leader   With the enemy's boot trampling the land,
                           you fell upon Saul with transforming power,
                           and he rose up to lead your people.

People [*singing*]   **Spirit of the living God,**
                           Strengthen us today.

Leader   In a time when the soul of your people
                           was dry and cracked, the prophet Joel
                           received a vision of a time when you would
                           be poured out on all the people of the world.

People [*singing*]   **Spirit of the living God,**
                           Give us dreams today.

Leader   At the River Jordan, the heavens opened
                           and you descended like a dove on Jesus,
                           anointing him to his sacrificial work.

People [*singing*]   **Spirit of the living God,**
                           Descend on us today.

Leader   At Pentecost you came down out of heaven
                           like the rush of a mighty wind, filling
                           all the house, and causing the people
                           to speak in other tongues.

People [*singing*]   **Spirit of the living God,**
                           Fill us here today.

Leader   Holy Spirit, whenever you fall upon your
                           people, we break out in worship and
                           witness, dancing and preaching, marching
                           and praying.

People [*singing*]   **Spirit of living God,**
                           Fall afresh on us.

Spirit of the living God,
Fall afresh on us.
Melt us, mold us, fill us, use us.
Spirit of the living God,
Fall afresh on us.

Prayer at the Table

140 Pastor Blessed are you, God most high,
forever working by your Spirit.

Elder 1 At creation your Spirit brought order out of chaos
and breathed into humankind the breath of life.
Your Spirit led Abraham and Sarah
to a land you had chosen and through them
called a people to be your very own.
On rulers and prophets your Spirit fell,
giving them power to lead your people.
When Mary waited before you,
your Spirit overshadowed her,
and she conceived a Son who would
save his people from their sins.

Elder 2 Your Spirit came to this Jesus Christ
who showed us life lived in its power:
unconditional love and compassion,
boldness in prayer,
the willingsness to die upon the cross.
At Pentecost your Spirit came like
the rush of a mighty wind,
filling the Apostles with power from on high,
making of their many tongues the one new
tongue of witness to you.

Pastor We give thanks to you, God of power and might,
that you send your Spirit to us at this
communion table, animating your people and
brooding over this bread and wine,
that we may receive again Christ's own life.
With these offerings we remember that
on the night when he was betrayed,
our Savior Jesus Christ took bread . . .

People **As we partake of these elements**
open our eyes to see the vision of your
presence here with us.
Strengthen us with spiritual food

so that we can prophesy with tongues of
love and transforming power.
Inspire all our thoughts, words, and actions
with your Holy Spirit that the world may be
renewed. Through Jesus Christ we pray. Amen.

Prayer After Communion
141 Thanks be to you, God of wind and fire,
for you are able to do immeasurably more
than all we can ask or think,
by the power at work among us.
To you be glory in the church and
in Christ Jesus. Amen.

Closing Words
142 May the Spirit go with you,
touching your tongue to preach like Peter,
bearing your feet on its wings to places of witness,
giving you the vision of a world in which
the hungry are fed, the lame walk, and
the handicapped are gathered into God's service.
May you be filled with power from on high
so that whatever you do, whatever you say,
whatever you are, abounds to the glory of God.

Trinity Sunday

In the Christian year the Sunday after Pentecost has centered on the meaning and significance of the Triune God. On this day we make explicit in our worship what is always implicit when Christians worship the one God of our faith. Much of our hymnody is formed by the motif of "God in three persons, Blessed Trinity." Even the character of music is a sign of the nature of God. Melody, harmony, rhythm have their distinct qualities; yet only when they are joined together in the living performance do they come to their full power.

Two hymns, theologically clear and musically strong, are especially appropriate for use on Trinity Sunday: "I Bind Unto Myself Today, The Strong Name of the Trinity," and "We All Believe in One True God." A more familiar hymn, "Holy, Holy, Holy, Lord God Almighty," praises "God in three persons, blessed trinity," without naming the persons of the Godhead. "Come, Thou

Almighty King" devotes each verse to the praise of one person: Almighty King, Incarnate Word, and Holy Comforter. The final stanza speaks to "the great One in Three." "God Whose Almighty Word" is a more subtle praise of the Trinity, referring to the three persons as wisdom, love, and might. "Holy God, We Praise Your Name" praises God and concludes with a powerful verse:

143 Though in essence only one:
Undivided God we claim you.
And, adoring, bend the knee
While we own thy mystery.

Trinity Sunday is a time when the Nicene Creed is most likely to be confessed in churches around the world. At a time of crisis, when the Christian faith was threatened by civil religion on the one hand and culture religion on the other, this confession emerged as the authentic sign of the apostolic faith. Ever since then, Christians have expressed their solidarity with primitive Christianity and with the church of the martyrs by reciting this ancient statement in their worship. Even though the use of this creed is not common in Disciples services, Trinity Sunday is a time when we can join with Christians around the world and across the ages in praising God by means of this ancient affirmation. (The text of this creed appears on page 131).

The eucharistic prayer on Trinity Sunday could be designed so that its trinitarian character is especially clear.

Paragraph 1: Thanksgiving for the creating, sustaining, and redeeming work of God in history.
Paragraph 2: Memorial of the special revelation of God through Christ, including the words of institution
Paragraph 3: Invocation of the transforming power of the Holy Spirit so that loaf and cup become carriers of the presence of the living Christ in the church and the church becomes the presence of Christ in the world.

World Communion Sunday

Most of the major commemorations of the Christian year are of ancient origin. The church does discern new occasions for celebration, one of which is World Communion Sunday. On this day

Christians around the world rejoice in the unity which has already been established in Christ, the unity which is most fully expressed by Holy Communion. By celebrating this sacrament, we are united with Jesus Christ and we are led to welcome one another even as Christ welcomes us.

The worldwide character of the church is made visible if the worship materials for World Communion Sunday are taken from other churches around the world. Our unity can be expressed by joining hands through the pews or in a large circle around the entire room.

144 A Communion Prayer for the Holy Spirit and Unity

> Pastor   Lord of the languages and nations,
> we offer you our thanks for creating
> a new unity among the divided peoples of the earth.
> **People   Through the cross of Christ**
> **you brought together Jew and Greek,**
> **male and female, slave and free.**
> **You gave them all to drink of the one Spirit**
> **and they became one great undivided church.**
> **We join our voices with Christians everywhere**
> **in praising you.**
> Pastor   O God, because you are One and desire that
> we be united, we bring to you this bread—
> many grains of wheat made into one loaf—
> and this wine—many grapes made into
> one cup of blessing.
> Pour out your Spirit afresh so that
> we may share in the body and blood of Christ.
> **People   May we who are many become one people**
> **as we partake of this one loaf.**
> **Restore to your divided church,**
> **as we drink from this cup,**
> **the unity that is our Savior's will.**
> **Amen.**

All Saints Day

All Saints Day, celebrated on November 1, complements World Communion Sunday because it recalls that our unity is across time as well as across space. Since the day itself usually comes on a week day, it is common practice to observe the previous Sunday as

a day to recall the great cloud of witnesses in whose succession we
serve and whose living memory is a source of inspiration for us.
All Saints Day is also an occasion to ponder the meaning of eternal
life and to call the roll of those in the congregation who have died
during the previous twelve months. The hymn identified with this
day is "For All the Saints."

145 A Litany of the Saints

Leader Gracious God, you are to be praised
for the women and men whose faithful
witness to your love inspires the
generations of your people:

All Abraham and Sarah, who believed your promise
even though they were old and barren;

Women Ruth, whose loyalty to Naomi became a
model for people of every time and place;

Men Isaiah of Jerusalem, who in time marked by
terror, proclaimed that the lion would
lie down with the lamb;

All Mary Magdalene, who ran from the tomb
crying out that Jesus was alive;

Women Paul of Tarsus, who was beaten
and shipwrecked while carrying the Gospel
to us, the Gentiles;

All Augustine, who when the cities of the world
were falling, saw the city of God;

Men Martin Luther, who spoke afresh
of salvation by grace alone through faith;

Women Sojourner Truth, who dreamed of
women and men, black and white, all of them free;

Men Thomas Campbell, Barton Stone,
and Alexander Campbell, who yearned
for a church with the vitality of
the New Testament church;

Women Mae Yoho Ward and other Disciples of our
own time who prayed and worked for
the life of the world to be shaped
by the power of the Spirit;

Men Martin Luther King, Jr., who prophesied of
the day when we all will be judged by the
content of character and not
by the color of skin;

Women Mother Teresa, who made her bed
       among the homeless, fed the hungry,
       and clothed the naked.
       [*The litany can be expanded to include saints
       known in the congregation.*]
All   As we recall the names of these witnesses,
       we pray that you will embolden us
       with the spirit of faithfulness
       which made them live for you.

Thanksgiving

In the Hebrew Scriptures the nation of Israel was one of the most important means of communion between God and God's people. Apostolic writers instruct the church to pray for rulers (1 Timothy 2:1-2), and through the generations churches have included days of national significance in their cycle of special commemorations. Services of worship on Thanksgiving Day or Eve are to be commended. The widespread observance of the Sunday before Thanksgiving provides a reasonable alternative for large numbers of people. Worship for this special day combines several themes in delicate balance. One of these basic ideas is thanksgiving for the productivity of the earth and for those who care for the earth. At the same time, we must confess our national and personal abuse of this great treasure and ask that God help us to develop a better stewardship of the natural resources that still abound. A second basic idea for this celebration is thanksgiving for this nation, with special attention to the vision of peace, freedom, responsibility, and abundance that has been foundational to our people. Yet, we must also confess to God how far short we are in our fulfillment of these ideals and ask for help to bring national life closer to the dream.

Christ the Cosmic Ruler

The political imagery which forms one of the motifs of Thanksgiving Day is even more prominent on the last Sunday of the church year. Traditionally, this day has been called the festival of Christ the King. One difficulty with this title is that king is a political term with diminished meaning in the modern world. Rather than conveying a sense of power over contemporary life, king sounds archaic and ceremonial. Even the untranslated Greek term *pantokrator* seems more potent, especially when it is linked with the powerful paintings of the resplendent Christ that one sees in Orthodox churches around the world. Christ the Cosmic Ruler is one attempt to express the idea that is foundational to this transitional Sunday. It centers on the universal sovereignty of Christ, a sovereignty which challenges our worship of the false gods of this world. This day sums up the meaning of the ministry of Jesus as dramatized from Christmas through Pentecost, and it points to the coming of Christ as judge and redeemer. Christ's sovereignty over the universe is already declared, but the full revelation we still await.

Christ's dominion was achieved during his lifetime not by the use of force but by suffering love; and in his teachings he stressed that in God's commonwealth preeminence comes from servanthood rather than from political power.

There is a long tradition in Judaism to celebrate in worship the enthronement of the king and the renewing of the nation's covenant with God. A similar approach can shape the celebration in Christian churches on this Sunday. The specific ideas of Christ's cosmic rule come into their sharpest focus at the communion table. Hymns such as "The Head That Once Was Crowned," "Lord, Enthroned in Heavenly Splendor," and "Look, Ye Saints, the Sight Is Glorious" interweave the themes of suffering and universal dominion. The prayers at the table can borrow language from the enthronement psalms, such as 93 and 95-99, from some of the hymns of the early church, such as Colossians 1:15-20 and Philippians 2:5-11, and from accounts of Jesus' trial and crucifixion, such as Mark 15:16-32, Matthew 27:27-44, Luke 23:6-11, and John 18:33-19:22. Revelation is a rich source of imagery for the rule of Christ, an imagery whose power is increased when read against the background of the suffering of the church for which Revelation was written (see especially 1:12-19; 4:1-5:14; 7:9-17; 11:15-19; and 15:1-8). The eucharistic prayer could include a congregational refrain patterned after the hymns and choruses of Revelation:

146 Worthy is the Lamb who was slain
  to receive power and wealth
  and wisdom and might and
  honor and glory and blessing.
  Hallelujah! For the Lord our God
  the Almighty reigns.

The idea of investing Christ with authority and power can be intensified if the worship includes actions that represent this enthronement. In the procession at the beginning of the service or in the procession when the offering is brought to the communion table, signs of Christ's sovereignty could also be carried and displayed while the people sing a hymn that exalts Christ's cosmic rule. A cross lifted high over the heads of the people or a globe of the world are examples.

147 A Communion Prayer of Thanksgiving for Justice and Mercy

Leader God of mercy and justice,
Source of life and salvation,
the whole world declares your glory!
Each day you renew the work of creation.
Every day you breathe in us the breath of life.

People **We give thanks for your justice
which holds us to what is right and true;
for your mercy which forgives and renews us
when we fall short;
for your promise, spoken by the prophets,
of a day when love and peace shall prevail.**

Leader Most of all we thank you for Christ Jesus,
who took the form of a servant,
died for us on the cross,
and was raised from the dead
that we might have new life.

People **We give thanks for people
who at other times and places have
followed Christ faithfully, doing justice,
giving love, praising your name,
whose lives are joined with ours at this table.**

All Eternal God, you are blessed, now and forever.
Amen.

Worship Resources for the Season After Pentecost

Greetings

148 Leader The Lord says, Fear not, for I am with you.
People **Do not be dismayed, for I am your God!**
Leader I will strengthen you.

People I will help you.
Leader I will uphold you with my right hand.
People I say to you, Fear not, for I am with you.
Leader Strengthened and unafraid, we worship God.

(Isaiah 41:10, 13)

149 Voice 1 Where could I go to escape your spirit?
Where could I flee from your presence?
Voice 2 If I climb the heavens, you are there;
there, too, if I lie in Sheol.
Voice 1 If I fly to the point of sunrise,
or westward across the sea,
your hand would still be guiding me,
your right hand holding me.
Voice 2 If I ask darkness to cover me
and light to become night around me,
the darkness would not be dark to you;
night would be as light as day.

(Psalm 139:7-12; JB)

The previous elements were based on scripture; the following illustrate opening words that are based on the life experience of the congregation and its people.

150 Leader We come to worship God,
yet we are distracted by our other callings:
People The bicycle's flat tire, the unmade bed;
schoolwork due tomorrow;
headlines in the morning news.
Leader Friends, give all these things to God,
for God embraces all of life.

151 Leader We come to give thanks to God!
People For the good world,
for things great and small,
for seen and unseen splendors.
Leader For human life and relationships shared.
People For work to do and strength to do it.
Leader For marriage and the mystery of flesh made one.
People For the energy and curiosity of children.
Leader For the high hopes and brave vision of the young.
People For wisdom deepened by experience.

Leader   For the Gospel making us alive.
People   Thanks be to God.

The following resources illustrate additional ways of developing greetings, opening sentences, and calls to worship. Number 152 uses a programatic theme, the installation of officers, as a way of organizing the call to worship. Number 153 is based on the text of a hymn which would be sung later in the service. Number 154 combines the leader's speaking with the choir's singing, using material drawn from the Psalms and from a hymn.

152 People   Bless, O servants of the Lord,
bless the name of the Lord.
On this day of installation,
bless the name of the Lord.
Leader 1   Elders, spiritual leaders of the congregation,
bless the Lord.
Leader 2   Deacons, servants of the table,
bless the Lord.
Leader 1   Teachers of the Christian faith,
bless the Lord.
Leader 2   President and officers,
bless the Lord.
Leader 1   Leaders of committees and groups,
bless the Lord.
          [*Other leaders may be added*]
Leader 2   All the household of faith,
women and men, old and young,
bless the Lord.
People   Bless, O servants of the Lord,
bless the name of the Lord.

153 With creating love, God made the world
and calls us into it.
With redeeming power and healing love,
God stills us.
With gracious mercy, God keeps us
from morning dawn to evening twilight.
With grateful song, let us give this
great God praise and glory.

154 Leader   I will bless you, God!

	You fill the world with awe! You dress yourself in light, rich, majestic light.
Choir	Light of light eternal, All things pentrating. For your rays our soul is waiting.
Leader	To you, O Lord, we lift up our souls.
Choir	As the tender flowers, willingly unfolding to the sun their faces holding.
Leader	My soul, bless the Lord! All my being, bless God's holy name!
Choir	Ever so would we do, Light from you obtaining, Strength to serve you gaining.

(Leader's texts are drawn from Psalms 104:1-2; 86:4; 103:1; the congregation's responses are taken from the hymn "God Himself Is With Us.")

Other biblical texts that can be adapted for use in this part of the service include the following items from the Psalms: 29:1-2; 34:1-3; 48:1; 66:1; 81:1; 95:1-2; 98:4-6; 100:1-2; 100:4-5; 103:21-22; 105:1; 105:2-3; 106:1; 107:31-32; 111:1; 113:1-2; 122:1; 135:1-3; 146:1-2; 147:1; 147:7-8; 148:1-2; 148:11-12; 149:1; 150:1-2, 6. The apostolic greeting, much used by Paul, can be adapted for use in services today. Examples can be found in Romans 16:20; 1 Corinthians 1:3; 2 Corinthians 1:3-4; Galatians 1:3-5; 1 Timothy 1:2b; 1 Peter 1:2b; 2 Peter 1:2; Jude 2. The example below is from Romans.

155 Leader   The grace of the Lord Jesus Christ be with you.
     People   And also with you.

Opening Prayers

The language of public prayer can be shaped by several sources as the following opening prayers illustrate. Number 156 employs themes drawn from Isaiah 40:10, 13; when compared with greeting Number 148, this prayer shows how one passage can contribute language for two parts of the same service. Prayers numbered 157, 158, and 159 are also based on biblical passages. Number 160 is suggested by a hymn, "Joyful, Joyful, We Adore Thee," which could also be used in the service. Number 161, taken from James Weldon Johnson's *God's Trombones*, illustrates that prayers and other excerpts from literature may be adapted for use in public worship. When using excerpts from other sources, leaders of worship should acknowledge their indebtedness.

156 We praise you, Great I Am,
for you are constantly with us.
Because you are our God,
we confidently look to you for strength
and help in this hour of worship.
Uphold us in your right hand
so that we may never be afraid
but will always serve you boldly and gladly.
Through our Savior Jesus Christ.

157 Liberating God,
we come into your presence
imprisoned, in hope of freedom,
hungry,in need of food,
sojourners, in search of a home.
Through your Word, give us freedom.
At your table, nourish us with the bread of life.
In your presence, give us an eternal home.
In the name of Jesus Christ, we pray.

158 God of light,
in whom there is no darkness at all:
by your Word you divide night from day
and cause the sun to shed its light
and warmth over all the earth.
Speak to us now, we pray, and take
away the night of doubt, fear, and death.
As the morning sun dispels the shadows,
may the light of your truth dispel
the shadows of envy, greed, and injustice.
May we live this and every hour
in the light of our Savior, Jesus Christ.

159 Blessed God, when Jesus spoke
your Word Zacchaeus was forgiven;
and at his healing touch Lazarus
was restored to life.

We pray that you will work in us
your miracles of love and redemption.
Send us home in right relationships
with you and one another.
Free us with your Word of forgiveness.
Lift us to life by the power of your Spirit.
Through Jesus Christ we pray.

160 God of life,
our hearts unfold like flowers before you.
We join the stars and angels singing around you.
You alone are the well-spring of the joy of living.
In this place we rejoice in you.
Lead us in our worship to sing
the triumph song of life.

161 O Lord, we come this morning
Knee-bowed and body-bent
Before thy throne of grace.
O Lord—this morning—
Bow our hearts beneath our knees,
And our knees in some lonesome valley.
We come this morning—
Like empty pitchers to a full fountain,
With no merits of our own.
O Lord—open up a window of heaven,
And lean out far over the battlements of glory,
And listen this morning.

Prayers of Confession
162 Most merciful God, we confess
that we have sinned against you
in thought, word, and deed,
by what we have done, and by what
we have left undone.
We have not loved you with our whole heart;
we have not loved our neighbors as ourselves.
We are truly sorry and we humbly repent.
For the sake of your Son Jesus Christ

have mercy on us and forgive us;
that we may delight in your will,
and walk in your ways,
to the glory of your name. Amen.

163 Leader   Lord God of all creation, hear our prayer.
                With dynamite and bulldozer we gouge the earth
                with no consideration for the years to come.
People   **God of the earth, forgive us.**
Leader   With automobiles beyond the counting
                we fill the sky with smog until darkness
                hangs over the land.
People   **God of sun and moon and sky, forgive us.**
Leader   With burned-out rockets and dead satellites
                we litter the heavens with debris that will
                remain for generations.
People   **God of the spinning planets, forgive us.**
Leader   Crazed by power and fear, we smash the atom
                and create engines to destroy all creation.
People   **Lord of life, forgive us.**
Leader   By your grace, revealed in Jesus Christ,
                restore us to our right minds.
People   **God of this fertile world, restore us
                to partnership with life. Amen.**

Responses of Praise
    Responses of praise, especially those that are trinitarian, can be
found in hymns already familiar to the congregation. These brief
musical elements can be used in place of *The Gloria*, or as responses
to the reading of scripture.

164 Holy, holy, holy, Lord God Almighty!
All your works shall praise your name
in earth and sky and sea;
Holy, holy, holy, Merciful and mighty!
God in three persons, blessed Trinity!
("Holy, Holy, Holy, Lord God Almighty")

165 Holy, holy, holy, Lord God of hosts!
Heaven and earth are full of thee!

Heaven and earth are praising thee!
O Lord most high.
("Day Is Dying in the West")

166 Alleluia! Alleluia! Glory be to God on high;
Alleluia! To the Savior who has won the victory;
Alleluia! To the Spirit, Fount of love and sanctity.
Alleluia! Alleluia! To the Triune Majesty.
("Alleluia! Alleluia! Hearts to Heaven and Voices Raise")

Affirmations of Faith
The oldest confession of faith outside of Scripture still in continuous use is the Apostles' Creed. Dating from the early third century, it developed from the baptismal liturgy used in Rome and still gives a beautiful, simple, but comprehensive expression of the core of the Christian faith.

167 I believe in God, the Father almighty,
    creator of heaven and earth.
    I believe in Jesus Christ, his only Son, our Lord.
    He was conceived by the power of the Holy Spirit
    and born of the Virgin Mary.
    He suffered under Pontius Pilate,
    was crucified, died, and was buried.
    He descended to the dead.
    On the third day he rose again.
    He ascended into heaven,
    and is seated at the right hand of the Father.
    He will come again to judge the living and the dead.
    I believe in the Holy Spirit,
    the holy catholic Church,
    the communion of saints,
    the forgiveness of sins,
    the resurrection of the body,
    and the life everlasting. Amen.

The Nicene Creed (text of 381 C.E.) is the most widely used of the great ecumenical confessions of faith. To confess it is not only to claim the faith which it sets forth but is to confess one's own solidarity with the universal church.

168 We believe in one God,
    the Father, the Almighty,

maker of heaven and earth,
of all that is, seen and unseen.

We believe in one Lord, Jesus Christ,
the only Son of God,
eternally begotten of the Father,
God from God, Light from Light,
true God from true God,
begotten, not made,
of one being with the Father.
Through him all things were made.
For us and for our salvation
he came down from heaven:
by the power of the Holy Spirit
he became incarnate from the Virgin Mary,
and was made man.
For our sake he was crucified under Pontius Pilate;
he suffered death and was buried.
On the third day he rose again
in accordance with the Scriptures;
he ascended into heaven
and is seated at the right hand of the Father.
He will come again in glory to judge the living
and the dead,
and his kingdom will have no end.
We believe in the Holy Spirit, the Lord, the giver of life,
who proceeds from the Father.
With the Father and the Son he is worshiped
and glorified.
He has spoken through the Prophets.
We believe in one holy catholic and apostolic Church.
We acknowledge one baptism for the forgiveness of sins.
We look for the resurrection of the dead,
and the life of the world to come. Amen.

The "Preamble" to *The Design for the Christian Church (Disciples of Christ)* was written in 1968 as an introduction to the document that reshaped the organizational life of our church. In a revised form, it is often used by Disciples to declare the Christian faith.

169 As members of the Christian Church,
We confess that Jesus is the Christ,

the Son of the living God,
and proclaim him Lord and Savior of the world.
In Christ's name and by his grace
we accept our mission of witness
and service to all people.
We rejoice in God,
maker of heaven and earth,
and in the covenant of love
which binds us to God and one another.
Through baptism into Christ
we enter into newness of life
and are made one with the whole people of God.
In the communion of the Holy Spirit,
we are joined together in discipleship
and in obedience to Christ.
At the table of the Lord
we celebrate with thanksgiving
the saving acts and presence of Christ.
Within the universal church,
we receive the gift of ministry
and the light of scripture.
In the bonds of Christian faith
we yield ourselves to God
that we may serve the One
whose kingdom has no end.
Blessing, glory, and honor
be to God forever. Amen.

In 1959 the United Church of Christ adopted a Statement which, like the Disciples' "Preamble," proclaims the Christian faith in the life of this church. The following revised form was approved for use in 1981:

170 We believe in you, O God, Eternal Spirit,
     God of our Savior Jesus Christ and our God,
     and to your deeds we testify.
     You call the worlds into being,
     create persons in your own image
     and set before each one the ways of
     life and death.
     You seek in holy love to save all people
     from aimlessness and sin.

You judge people and nations by your righteous will
declared through prophets and apostles.
In Jesus Christ, the man of Nazareth,
our crucified and risen Savior,
you have come to us
and shared our common lot,
conquering sin and death
and reconciling the world to yourself.
You bestow upon us your Holy Spirit,
creating and renewing the Church of Jesus Christ,
binding in covenant faithful people of all ages,
tongues and races.
You call us into your Church
to accept the cost and joy of discipleship,
to be your servants in the service of others,
to proclaim the gospel to all the world,
to resist the powers of evil,
to share in Christ's baptism and eat at his table,
to join him in his passion and victory.
You promise to all who trust you
forgiveness of sins and fullness of grace,
courage in the struggle for justice and peace,
your presence in trial and rejoicing,
and eternal life in your realm which has no end.
Blessing and honor, glory and power be unto you. Amen.

Scriptural Affirmations

Many passages of scripture sum up essential aspects of the
gospel and can become the basis for affirmations of faith. In addition to the two examples given below, several of the passages from
the list on p. 108 can be used in this way.

171   When we were still helpless,
at the time God chose,
Christ died for the wicked.
God has shown such great love for us
that while we were yet sinners
Christ died for us.
By this death we are now put right with God.
We were enemies of God, but God
has made us friends through the death of Christ.
Now that we are God's friends,

how much more will we be saved by Christ's life.
We rejoice because of what God has done
through our Lord Jesus Christ.

(Romans 5:6, 8-11; adapted from TEV)

172 Leader Remember that you were at one time
separated from Christ,
alienated from the commonwealth of Israel,
and strangers to the covenant of promise,
having no hope and without God in the world.
But now in Christ Jesus you who once were far off
have been brought near in the blood of Christ.

People **For he is our peace, who has made us both one,
and has broken down the dividing wall of
hostility by abolishing in his flesh the law
of commandments and ordinances that he might
create in himself one new people in place of two,
so making peace, and might reconcile us both
to God in one body through the cross,
thereby bringing the hostility to an end.**

Leader So then, you are no longer strangers and
sojourners but you are fellow citizens with
the saints and members of the household of God,
built upon the foundation of the apostles
and prophets, Christ Jesus himself being
the chief cornerstone.

(Ephesians 1:12-21)

Prayers of the People

173 With all our heart and mind,
let us pray to the Lord, saying,
Lord, hear our prayer.
For the church of Christ through all the world,
that it may be united in the gospel and
renewed in its witness and work,
let us pray to the Lord.
Lord, hear our prayer.
For the peace of the world and
the coming to justice among all its people,
let us pray to the Lord.
Lord, hear our prayer.
For those who suffer oppression or violence,

for those who hunger or have no hope,
that their oppressors will be made powerless
and their destitution be relieved,
let us pray to the Lord.
Lord, hear our prayer.
For those in our community who suffer
from illness, anxiety, or grief,
that they may be healed,
let us pray to the Lord.
Lord, hear our prayer.
For the earth which God created with
beauty and untold wealth,
that it may be restored to
its former glory,
let us pray to the Lord.
Lord, hear our prayer.
For our enemies and those who wish us harm,
for all whom we have wronged,
that reconciliation may come,
let us pray to the Lord.
Lord, hear our prayer.
For those who have died in the hope
of life eternal, let us pray to the Lord.
Lord, hear our prayer.
Into your hands, O God,
we commend all for whom we pray,
trusting in your mercy,
through Christ, our Savior and Friend.
Amen.

174 Eternal God, great Shepherd,
you call us by name and we follow you.
Because we know your voice,
we trust you to lead your flock
through the valley into green pastures.
Shepherd, in your loving kindness,
Hear our prayer.
We carry the heavy weight of our sins
for like sheep we have gone astray.
We want to choose our own path,
create our own oases, and
remain aloof from the needs of others.

We listen to voices other than yours,
and we are seduced by the promises
of wealth, power, and prestige.
Forgive us, dear God,
for we are truly sorry.
Speak your word of pardon,
and restore us in heart, mind, and body
to the place you have made for us.
Shepherd, in your loving kindness,
Hear our prayer.
We give you thanks, good Shepherd,
for the abundant gifts you give us,
and especially for . . . .
[*Here the prayer names specific items from
the life of the congregation and the life of
the world which are reasons for thanksgiving.*]
Shepherd, in your loving kindness,
Hear our prayer.
Because you have many sheep who are not of our fold,
we pray for. . . .
[*Here the prayer names the specific intercessions
that are appropriate for the day.*]
Shepherd, in your loving kindness,
Hear our prayer.
Shepherd of love, you spread a table before us.
Push us to the side so that there will be
room for the hungry who stand in line
[*Here the prayer names specific petitions
from the life of the congregation.*]
Shepherd, in your loving kindness,
Hear our prayer.
These and all our prayers, we offer to you
in the name of Jesus Christ,
to whom be glory forever and ever.
Amen.

Hymns and choruses often provide the language for the congregation to use in prayer. When their portion is sung, the prayer takes on greater intensity as it is offered to God. The following example uses a verse from a metrical version of Psalm 42, which can be sung to tunes in Common Metre.

175 Leader   God of summer's fullness,
you give us the sun to ripen crops,
trees for refreshing shade,
cool water for recreation,
yet they are not enough.
Hear us, we pray.

People   **As longs the deer for cooling streams,**
In parched and barren ways,
So longs my soul, O God, for thee
And thy refreshing grace.

Leader   Restless for purpose and meaning in life,
we give ourselves to things that do not satisfy,
to groups that serve no useful purpose,
to entertainment that warps our values
to relationships that manipulate and abuse,
to gods that are empty and false.
Hear us, we pray.

People   **As longs the deer for cooling streams,**
In parched and barren ways,
So longs my soul, O God, for thee
And thy refreshing grace.

Leader   God of mercy and compassion, we lift up to you
people who suffer in summer's heat:
those who swelter in substandard housing,
where no breeze stirs,
those whose fields are dry and hard,
those who wander in the streets,
those who are burned by the sun and by life.
O God, the needs are great,
and our efforts to help so small and withered.
Hear us, we pray.

People   **As longs the deer for cooling streams,**
In parched and barren ways,
So longs my soul, O God, for thee
And thy refreshing grace.

Leader   When thunderclouds roll and lightnings flash,
in the summer's sky and heat,
come with your quieting grace.
Fill us with song, like birds at dawn.
Hear us, gracious God, as we pray.

People   **As longs the deer for cooling streams,**
In parched and barren ways,

So longs my soul, O God, for thee
And thy refreshing grace.

Invitations to Communion

These examples of the invitation to communion show different approaches to composing them. Number 176, widely known in Disciples congregations, expresses the contrast between our unworthiness and the invitation of Christ. Number 177 uses the invitation to communion to express the evangelical center of the gospel, something which should be proclaimed somewhere in the service every Sunday. Number 178 shows how programatic aspects of church life can be used as part of the inspiration for the invitation to communion. Number 179 draws upon the harvest of wheat and grapes and suggests that communion is a harvest festival in the Christian life.

176　Let us come to the table of communion
　　　not because we must but because we may.
　　　Let us sit together in humility and thanksgiving
　　　rather than in pride or possessiveness.
　　　Let us confess, not that we are righteous,
　　　but that we love our Lord Jesus Christ
　　　and desire to remember him.
　　　Let us come, not that we are strong
　　　but that we are needy,
　　　not that we have any claim on Christ,
　　　but that he invites us to receive his grace
　　　and experience his presence.
　　　Let us worthily partake that he may be
　　　made known to us in the breaking of bread.

177　Are you alone and afraid?
　　　Come to the table and find Christ the friend.
　　　Are you broken in heart and body?
　　　Come to the table and find Christ the healer.
　　　Have you lost the power to do your work?
　　　Come to the table and find Christ the creator.
　　　Are you burdened by sin?
　　　Come to the table and meet Christ the savior.
　　　Are you dead to God?

Come to the table and meet Christ the living
presence of God.

178 Leader   Scattered from south to north,
and from west to east, we have come home.
After travel and recreation, study and
summer work, reunions with friends and family
we return to the patterns of normal life.

People   **Everywhere we went, and in everything
we did, Christ was with us.**

Leader   Now Christ invites us to this table
spread with his body and blood.
Let us come to this our true home
and to the reunion that has no ending.

179 Fruit hangs heavy on the vine.
Bread comes fresh from the oven.
Christ spreads the feast for you and me.
Bring your new wine and fresh bread.
Prepare the table for the living Lord
who makes every meal a sacrament of love.

Prayers at the Table

180 *A Prayer from the Disciple Tradition*
Most merciful heavenly Father,
in whose likeness we have been created
and by whose grace we have been redeemed;
with grateful hearts we approach this your table
to commemorate the sufferings of our dear Lord.
We thank you for your great love
which caused you to give us your only begotten Son
to redeem us from sin and death
through his own death for us.
And we thank you for the great privilege
of being numbered among his disciples
and counted worthy of a place at your table.
Assist us, we pray, our heavenly Father,
to partake of this bread and wine worthily,
discerning the Lord's body and blood;
and as we partake of these material emblems,
grant that we also may be partakers

of Christ's spirit and life,
so that, as he gave himself for us,
we may also give ourselves freely to your service
and to one another in acts of Christian love.
Give us, we pray, a realizing sense of your
spiritual presence with us in this institution,
that we may each be strengthened thereby;
and so go forward in life's duties,
stronger and purer for your service.
And grant us at last the unspeakable joy
of sitting down together
with the innumerable company of the redeemed
at the marriage supper of the Lamb
in your everlasting kingdom;
through Jesus Christ our Lord. Amen.

181 Leader　Eternal God, always and everywhere we give you
　　　　　　thanks for the life which comes from you.
　　　　　　Today as we are joined with our Savior
　　　　　　and each other at this communion table,
　　　　　　we offer you our heartfelt gratitude for the
　　　　　　good things that you have done for us.
　　　　　　In this time of silence, hear our prayers
　　　　　　of thanksgiving.

　　　　　　[Silent thanksgivings may be offered; brief prayers of thanks-
　　　　　　giving for life and for the new life in Jesus Christ may here be
　　　　　　spoken.]

　　Leader　Dear God, all of these prayers we gather
　　　　　　into one testimony of praise which
　　　　　　we offer to you with these gifts that
　　　　　　we place on your table.
　People　**Accept our gratitude, we pray,**
　　　　　　for the sake of your beloved Son Jesus Christ
　　　　　　who gave his life that we may have life with you.
　　Leader　By your Word and Holy Spirit,
　　　　　　bless this bread and wine
　　　　　　that we who share this meal
　　　　　　may become the body of Christ in the world.
　　　　　　Through us may people everywhere be
　　　　　　given cause to offer their own thanks to you.

People **And to you, Holy God, Father, Son, and Holy
Spirit, be all honor and praise forever and ever.
Amen.**

182 Leader O God, our Savior, in tender mercy
you love us more deeply than we can ever know.
You gave life to humankind and have kept
us going with every breath we draw.

People **When early generations rebelled against your will,
you offered forgiveness through the law
and the ceremonies of worship.
When the world was ready you sent
your own Word in human form,
Jesus the son of Mary,
so that everyone could see your grace and truth
and know your saving love.**

Leader We praise you that he lived a life like ours,
except that he did not sin,
and that he gave his life for us.
We give you thanks that this same Jesus
now sits at your side praying for us.
In deepest gratitude we cry out:

People **Holy, holy, holy Lord, God of power and might,
heaven and earth are full of your glory,
Hosanna in the highest.**

Leader Holy God, by the power of your living Spirit
bless this bread and wine and your people
who gather around this table.
Unite us with Jesus in your presence.
Join our own prayers, which we offer in
this time of silence, with those that
Jesus offers on our behalf.

[*Silent intercessions may be offered; brief intercessions for the
world, the universal church and its leaders, and the congregation may here be spoken.*]

Leader All of these prayers, spoken and unspoken,
we offer to you, O God, in obedient love.
Joined with Christ and the heavenly host,
we dare to speak the words that Jesus taught:
(Our Father . . .)

183 Blessed are you,
eternal and glorious God!
We remember with joy
that you are the Creator,
the Fountain of life,
the Source of all goodness.
You have made us,
women and men,
in your holy image.
You called Israel to be your people
and delivered them from bondage.
When the time had come,
your Word became flesh in Jesus Christ,
who took upon himself our nature
and suffered death upon the cross
so that we would be forgiven and made new.
At this table, we remember with thanksgiving
his life and saving work:
how he proclaimed
comfort to the afflicted,
freedom to the oppressed,
joy to the sorrowful,
good news to the poor.
We celebrate his resurrection,
his continuing presence with us,
and the promise of his coming in glory
to complete the work of redemption.
Together with Christians
of every race and culture
we covenant anew to live
no longer for ourselves
but for Jesus
who died and rose for us.
Blessed are you, great God,
now and forever. Amen.

Closing Words

184 The grace of the Lord Jesus Christ and the love of God and
the fellowship of the Holy Spirit be with you all. (2 Corinthians
13:14)

185 Be watchful, stand firm in your faith, be courageous, be

strong. Let all that you do be done in love. (1 Corinthians
16:13-14)

186   The peace of God, which passes all understanding, keep your
hearts and minds in Christ Jesus. (Philippians 4:7)

187   The Lord be with your spirit. Grace be with you. (2 Timothy
4:22)

188   Put to death that which is earthly in you:
immorality, impurity, and covetousness.
As God's chosen ones, put on:
compassion, kindness, and patience.
Above all these, put on love.
And whatever you do, in word or deed,
do everything in the name of the Lord Jesus,
giving thanks to God. (from Colossians 3)

189   The blessing of the God of Sarah and Abraham,
the blessing of the Son, born of Mary,
the blessing of the Holy Spirit who broods
over us as a mother over her children,
be with you all.

Communion Prayers from
the Ecumenical Church

One of the major steps in the movement toward Christian
unity is the creating of liturgies that can be used by churches
which have previously worshiped in isolation from one another.
The three sets of prayers that follow have been developed in this
time when divided Christians are rediscovering the unity that
Christ gives. Number 190 was developed by the commission on
worship of the Consultation on Church Union. Published in 1969,
it has been given high marks by theologians and has been much
used in services of worship, especially by churches that participate
in COCU. Number 191 is often called *The Lima Liturgy* because it
was first used at a meeting in Lima, Peru, in 1982. Based on the
theological achievement of the document *Baptism, Eucharist and Ministry,* the liturgy brings together essential eucharistic themes from

the international Christian community. It is especially suited to a festival day. At times such as World Communion Sunday or the Week of Prayer for Christian Unity, it would be a strong symbol of a local congregation's solidarity with the global church. Number 192 was created by people involved in a different form of ecumenism, in the struggle for liberation. By using this prayer from the Latin American context, Christians in North America enter more fully into the gospel call to freedom in Jesus Christ.

190 *The Consultation on Church Union*
Pastor   We give you thanks,
holy Father, almighty and eternal God,
always and everywhere,
through Jesus Christ your Son our Lord,
by whom you made the world
and all things living and beautiful.
We bless you for your continual love and care
for every creature.
We praise you for forming us in your image
and calling us to be your people.
Though we rebelled against your love,
you did not abandon us to sin
but sent to us prophets and teachers
to lead us into the way of salvation.
Above all, we give you thanks
for the gift of Jesus your only Son,
who is the way, the truth, and the life.
In the fullness of time
he took upon himself our nature;
and by the obedience of his life,
his suffering on the cross,
and his resurrection from the dead,
he has delivered us from the way of sin and death.
We praise you that he now reigns with you
in glory and ever prays for us.
We thank you for the Holy Spirit
who leads us into truth,
defends us in adversity,
and unites us out of every people
in one holy Church.
Therefore with the whole company of saints
in heaven and on earth,

we worship and glorify you, God most holy,
and we sing with joy:

People   **Holy, holy, holy Lord God of hosts,**
heaven and earth are full of your glory.
Glory be to you, O Lord most High.

Pastor   Holy Father, most glorious and gracious God,
we give you thanks
that our Savior Jesus Christ,
before he suffered,
gave us this memorial of his sacrifice,
until his coming again:
For in the night in which he was betrayed
[*the words of institution are said*]

People   **His death, O God, we proclaim.**
His resurrection we declare.
His coming we await.
Glory be to you, O Lord.

Pastor   Heavenly Father, show forth among us
the presence of your life-giving Word and
Holy Spirit to sanctify us and your whole church
through these holy mysteries.
Grant that all who share the communion
of the Body and Blood of our Savior Jesus Christ
may be one in him
and remain faithful in love and hope
until that perfect feast with him
in the joy of his eternal Kingdom.

People   **Gracious Father, accept with favor**
this our sacrifice of praise
which we now present with these holy gifts.
We offer to you ourselves,
giving you thanks for calling us to your service,
as your own people,
through the perfect offering
of your Son Jesus our Lord;
By whom, and with whom and in whom,
in the unity of the Holy Spirit
all honor and glory be to you,
Father Almighty, now and forever.
Amen.

As our Savior Christ has taught us, we dare to say,
[*The Lord's Prayer is said*]

Pastor   The bread which we break,
          is it not a sharing in the body of Christ?
**People Because there is one bread,
          we who are many are one body,
          for we all partake of the one bread.**
Pastor   The wine which we drink,
          is it not a sharing in the blood of Christ?
**People The cup which we bless
          is the communion in the blood of Christ.**
Pastor   Alleluia! Christ our Passover is sacrificed for us.
People Therefore, let us keep the feast. Alleluia!
Pastor   Blessed is he who comes in the name of the Lord.
People Hosanna in the highest.
Pastor   The gifts of God for the people of God.

191 *The Lima Liturgy*

Invitation to the Table
Blessed are you, Lord God of the universe,
you are the giver of this bread,
fruit of the earth and of human labor,
let it become the bread of life.
People   Blessed be God, now and for ever!

Blessed are you, Lord God of the universe,
you are the giver of this wine,
fruit of the vine and of human labor,
let it become the window of the eternal kingdom.
People   Blessed be God, now and for ever!

As the grain once scattered in the field
and the grapes once dispersed on the hillside
are now reunited on this table,
in bread and wine,
so, Lord, may your whole church
soon be gathered together
from the corners of the earth into your kingdom.
People   Maranatha! Come, Lord Jesus.

Dialogue

Pastor   The Lord be with you.
People   And also with you.
Pastor   Lift up your hearts.
People   We lift them to the Lord.
Pastor   Let us give thanks to the Lord our God.
People   It is right to give our thanks and praise.

Preface

Truly it is right and good to glorify you,
at all times and in all places,
to offer you our thanksgiving, O Lord, Holy Father,
Almighty and Everlasting God.
Through your living Word you created all things,
and pronounced them good.
You made human beings in your own image,
to share your life and reflect your glory
as the Way, the Truth, and the Life.
He accepted baptism and consecration as your servant
to announce the good news to the poor.
At the last supper
Christ bequeathed to us the Eucharist,
that we should celebrate the memorial
of the cross and resurrection,
and receive his presence as the Bread of Life.
Wherefore, Lord, with the angels
and all the saints,
we proclaim and sing your glory:

Sanctus and Benedictus

People   Holy, Holy, Holy Lord, God of power and might,
heaven and earth are full of your glory.
Hosanna in the highest.
Blessed is he who comes in the name of the Lord.
Hosanna in the highest.

Invocation I (Epiclesis I)

O God, Lord of the universe,
you are holy and your glory is beyond measure.
Upon our Eucharist send the life-giving Spirit,
who spoke by Moses and the prophets,
who overshadowed the Virgin Mary with grace,

who descended upon Jesus in the River Jordan
and upon the apostles on the day of Pentecost.
May the outpouring of this Spirit of fire
transfigure this thanksgiving meal
that this bread and wine may become for us
the body and blood of Christ.
People   Come, Creator Spirit.

Institution
May this Creator Spirit accomplish the words
of your beloved Son
who in the night on which he was betrayed . . .
[*the Words of Institution are spoken*]

People   Your death, Lord Jesus, we proclaim!
          Your resurrection we celebrate!
          Your coming in glory we await!

Remembrance (Anamnesis)
Wherefore, Lord,
we celebrate today the memorial of our redemption:
we recall the birth and life of your Son among us,
his baptism by John,
his last meal with the apostles,
his death and descent to the abode of the dead;
we proclaim Christ's resurrection and ascension in glory,
where as our Great High Priest
he ever intercedes for all people;
and we look for his coming at the last.
United in Christ's priesthood,
we present to you this memorial:
Remember the sacrifice of your Son
and grant to people everywhere the benefits
of Christ's redemptive work.
People   Maranatha, the Lord comes!

Invocation (Epiclesis II)
Behold, Lord, this Eucharist
which you yourself gave to the Church
and graciously receive it,
as you accept the offering of your Son
whereby we are reinstated in your covenant.

As we partake of Christ's body and blood,
fill us with the Holy Spirit
that we may be one single body
and one single spirit in Christ,
a living sacrifice to the praise of your glory.
People   Come, Creator Spirit!

Conclusion
Through Christ, with Christ, in Christ,
all honor and glory is yours,
Almighty God and Father,
in the unity of the Holy Spirit,
now and for ever.
People   Amen.

The Lord's Prayer
Pastor   United by one baptism
             in the same Holy Spirit and
             the same Body of Christ,
             we pray as God's sons and daughters:
People   Our Father . . .

The Peace
Leader   Lord Jesus Christ, you told your apostles:
             Peace I leave with you, my peace I give to you.
             Look not on our sins but
             on the faith of your church.
             In order that your will be done,
             grant us always this peace and guide us
             toward the perfect unity
             of your kingdom for ever.
People   Amen.

Leader   The peace of the Lord be with you always.
People   And also with you.
Leader   Let us give one another a sign of
             reconciliation and peace.
             [*People exchange signs and words of peace*]

The Breaking of the Bread
Leader   The bread which we break
             is the communion of the body of Christ.

The cup of blessing for which we give thanks
is the communion in the Blood of Christ.

People **Lamb of God, you take away the sin of the world.**
Have mercy on us.
Lamb of God, you take away the sin of the world,
have mercy on us.
Lamb of God, you take away the sin of the world,
grant us peace.
[*The people partake of the loaf and the cup*]

Prayer After Communion

Leader   In peace let us pray to the Lord:
O Lord our God, we give you thanks
for uniting us by baptism in the Body of Christ
and for filling us with joy in the eucharist.
Lead us toward the full visible unity of your church
and help us to treasure all the signs of reconciliation
you have granted us.
Now that we have tasted of the banquet
you have prepared for us in the world to come,
may we all one day share together
the inheritance of the saints
in the life of your heavenly city,
through Jesus Christ, your Son, our Lord,
who lives and reigns with you
in the unity of the Holy Spirit,
ever one God, world without end.

People **Amen.**

192 A Mexican Eucharistic Prayer

Indeed, Father, how could we possibly not thank you
for the earth you have given to us!
With joy we praise you
for the high mountains and their trees,
for the rushing waters of Usumacinta and Grijalva
which give energy and fruitfulness,
for the forests so luxuriant in foliage
for the fertile plains and the tropical abundance.

We remember, Father,
how in ancient times you proved your faithfulness
by choosing for your own, from all the peoples,
a people humiliated and oppressed by Pharaoh
even to death.
Father, in our own people, too,
once oppressed in slavery and serfdom,
then robbed of its fruitful land,
its forests and minerals,
fighting heroically in resistance,
ready even to die in blood uprisings,
in this people, too, we recognize
the elect people of your immeasurable
bounty and goodness.
In the symphony of tomorrow
all languages in heaven and on earth
sing your praise and call upon you.
People   Holy, holy, holy. . . .

Indeed, Father, you are truly Holy
for you renounced power in sending your son to us
to share our suffering and our hard daily toil.
He came into the world in poverty,
in a distant corner of the Empire.
He knew failure.
He demonstrated to us his power
by resolutely challenging the rulers of the Temple
and the representative of the Emperor,
When he was betrayed
and freely chose the way of death
he took the bread, gave thanks and broke it.
We offer to you this bread
for the hunger which still devastates our earth,
for the torturing of prisoners,
for the undeclared deaths of
the kidnapped and the disappeared.
Raising this cup of joy,
we also proclaim his resurrection,
and celebrate the victorious struggles
through which our people have passed
on their long way of suffering,
in the unshakable confidence

that one day we shall thereby achieve
a more just and fraternal community.
Righteous Father,
send upon us the Spirit of Jesus
that all we who share this bread
and drink from this cup
may be united in the work of preparation
for the Feast of the Free People
for which your son laid down his own life.
In sharing this bread and drinking from this cup,
we join the company of
the day-laborers with a thousand cares
the campesinos [*peasants*] without land or harvest,
the workers without work,
the joiners without wood,
the women robbed of their dignity,
the humiliated and abandoned wife,
all who are persecuted for justice and brotherhood's sake,
and all those others who have sacrificed themselves
in the endeavour to turn our native land
into a tiny part of the Kingdom of your son.
In this communion, we await, O Father,
the resurrection which is to come
and which has already begun in history.

A COLLECTION OF
PSALM RESPONSES

This collection presents portions of twenty-two psalms which are widely used in the Sunday service. They have been newly translated so that the English will be faithful to the Hebrew text, use an English style that is easily recited or sung in worship, show respect for God's name, and be as inclusive as the Hebrew text will allow.

The church uses psalms as the foundation for its praise and prayer because Christian worship is rooted in the life of Israel. These prayer poems were created by Jews and were the primary language of their devotion. Jesus used these ancient psalms, and when Christians pray these same words we are put in touch with Jesus' own inner life of piety and worship. Furthermore, the psalms express a wide range of emotion—wonder, fear, frustration, trust, rage, resignation, joy, hope—all of which are part of our Christian experience before God.

Even in this contemporary translation, using inclusive language, these psalms carry the flavor of ancient times. They talk about exotic places and people. The images come from a culture in which shepherds were commonplace and kings were the people of power and splendor. In our worship we will use other figures of speech, drawn from our own times. Yet these ancient metaphors still speak. They tell of God who loves and cares for us; and they also portray God as the majestic ruler of all that is and can ever be.

In worship the psalms are used several ways. The most common is to select brief portions for opening sentences, invitations to the offering, and other brief statements of devotion. Psalms are widely used as part of the service of the Word, usually read in unison or recited in a responsive pattern, so that the congregation can participate vocally in the reading and hearing of God's word.

The psalms have often served as the inspiration for hymns, and often such a hymn may be sung as the psalm for the day.

The psalms are similar to hymns and they deserve to be sung. In many churches the congregation sings or says the *response* and a solo voice or ensemble sings the verses. Whether said or sung, it is common practice for a leader of worship to recite the response which is then repeated by the congregation. If a leader or ensemble recites the psalm verses, the congregation may repeat the response between verses. At the close of the psalm the response is said or sung one more time.

The number of psalm portions in this collection is small and the selections are brief, which means that many of these verses will be used three or four times during a year. Gradually worshipers will develop a familiarity with these classic poems of devotion. The following table suggests how these twenty-two psalms may be keyed to the seasons of the church year.

Advent

(1) 25:4-5b, 8-9, 10 and 14
(2) 85:8ab and 9, 10-11, 12-13

Christmas

98:1, 2-3b, 3c-4, 5-6

Epiphany

72:1-2, 7-8, 10-11, 12-13

Lent

(1) 51:1-2, 3-4, 10-11, 12 and 15
(2) 91:1-2, 10-11, 12-13, 14 and 15c-16
(3) 130:1-2, 3-4, 5-6b, 6c-8

Holy Week

22:7-8, 16-17a, 18-19, 22-23

Easter Vigil

136:1-3, 4-6, 7-9, 24-26

Easter

(1) 66:1-3a, 6-7a, 16 and 20
(2) 118:1-2, 15c-17, 22-23

Ascension
47:1-2, 5-6, 7-8

Pentecost
104:1ab and 24cd, 27-29a, 29b-30, 31 and 33-4

Seasons of Epiphany and Pentecost
(1) 19:7, 8, 9, 10
(2) 27:1, 4, 13-14
(3) 34:1-2, 3-4, 5-6, 7-8
(4) 63:1, 2-3, 4-5, 7-8
(5) 95:1-2, 6-7, 8-9
(6) 100:1-2, 3, 4-5
(7) 103:1-2, 3-5, 8-10, 11-13
(8) 145:1-2, 8-9, 10-11, 13c-14

Last Weeks of Pentecost
122:1-2, 3-4ab, 4c-5b, 6-7, 8-9

When reproducing any of these psalms in worship bulletins, the following credit line fulfills legal requirements. "Psalm text from *Consultation on a Liturgical Psalter* copyright 1984, International Commission on English in the Liturgy, Inc. All rights reserved."

Psalm 19

Response
Lord, you have the words of everlasting life.

Verses

God's perfect law
revives the soul.
God's stable rule
guides the simple.

God's just demands
delight the heart.
God's clear commands
sharpen vision.

God's faultless decrees
stand for ever.
God's right judgments
keep their truth.

Their worth is more than gold,
the purest gold.
Their taste richer than honey,
sweet from the comb.

(19:7, 8, 9, 10)

Psalm 22

Response
God, my God, why have you abandoned me?

Verses

All who see me jeer at me,
sneer at me, wagging their heads.
"He relied on God. God will help him!
Let God who loves him save him!"

There are dogs all around me,
a pack of villains corners me.
They tear my hands and feet.
I can count all my bones.

They take what I wore;
they roll dice for my clothes.
You, Lord, do not stay far off.
You, my Strength, be quick to help.

I will proclaim your name to my people.
I will praise you in the assembly.
Praise God, all who fear God.
Honor God, people of Jacob.

(22:7-8, 16-17a, 18-19, 22-23)

[*Note: Jesus quoted this psalm on the cross; and by praying these words during Holy Week Christians identify themselves with Jesus' suffering.*]

Psalm 25
Response
Lord, I give myself to you.

Verses

Teach me how to live,
Lord, show me the way.
Steer me toward your truth,
you my saving God.

Good and just is the Lord,
guiding those who stray.
God leads the poor,
pointing out their path.

God's ways are faithful love
for those who keep the covenant.
God confides in you
to show what covenant means.
        (25:4-5b, 8-9, 10 and 14)

Psalm 27
Response
The Lord is my saving light.

Verses

The Lord is my saving light;
what should I fear?
God a fort around me;
what should I dread?

One thing I ask the Lord,
one thing I seek:
to live in the house of God
every day of my life;
caught up in God's beauty,
at prayer in God's temple.

I expect to see
how good God is

while I am still alive.
Trust in the Lord: be strong.
Be brave. Trust in the Lord.
>   (27:1, 4, 13-14)

Psalm 34

Response
I will never stop thanking God.

Verses
I will never stop thanking God,
with constant words of praise.
My soul will boast of God;
the poor will hear me and be glad.

Join me in praising the Lord;
together tell of God's name.
I asked; the Lord responded,
freed me from all my fears.

Turn to God, be bright with joy;
you shall never be let down.
I begged; God heard,
and took my burdens from me.

God's angel defends the faithful,
guards them on every side.
Drink in the richness of God,
trust the Lord for your strength.
>   (34:1-2, 3-4, 5-6, 7-8)

Psalm 47

Response
**God ascends the hill
to cheers and trumpet blasts.**

Verses
All peoples, clap your hands,
shout with joy to God.
For God above is awesome,
king of all the earth.

God ascends the hill
to cheers and trumpet blasts.
Sing out your praise to God,
to the king sing out your praise.

For God rules the earth;
sing praise with all your skill.
God rules over nations,
high on the sacred throne.
(47:1-2, 5-6, 7-8)

Psalm 51

Response
**Have mercy, tender God,
forget that I defied you.**

Verses

Have mercy, tender God,
forget that I defied you.
Wash away my sin.
Cleanse me from my guilt.

I know my evil well,
it stares me in the face,
evil done against you
before your very eyes.

Creator, reshape my heart.
God, steady my spirit.
Do not cast me aside
stripped of your holy spirit.

Bring back my joy: save me.
Support me, free my spirit.
Lord, give me words
and I will shout your praise.
(51:1-2, 3-4, 10-11, 12 and 15)

Psalm 63

Response
God, my God, my soul thirsts for you
like a dry and weary land.

Verses

God, my God, you I crave;
my soul thirsts for you,
my body aches for you,
like a dry and weary land.

Let me gaze on you in your temple,
a vision of strength and glory.
Your love is better than life;
my speech is full of praise.

I give you a lifetime of worship;
my hands lifted in prayer.
I feast at a rich table;
my lips sing out your praise.

You have been my help;
I rejoice beneath your wings.
Yes, I cling to you;
your right hand holds me fast.
      (63:1, 2-3, 4-5, 7-8)

Psalm 66

Response
All earth, shout with joy to God.

Verses

All earth, shout with joy to God!
Sing to the glory of the Name!
Give glorious praise!
Say, "How awesome your works!"

God turned sea into land,
they crossed the river on foot.
Let us rejoice then in God,
who rules for ever with might.

Come, listen, all who fear God,
as I tell you what happened to me.
God did not reject my plea,
but pledged me constant love.
(66:1-3a, 6-7a, 16 and 20)

Psalm 72

Response
**Let the glory of God
fill the world!**

Verses

God, give your king
your sense of what is just;
make him a judge like you,
fair to us the powerless.

May justice sprout in his time,
peace till the moon is no more.
May he rule from sea to sea,
from the River to the ends of the earth.

Kings from Tarshish and the islands
will bring their riches to him.
All kings will bow before him,
all peoples serve him.

He will rescue the poor at their call,
those no one speaks for.
Those no one cares for
he hears and will save.
(72:1-2, 7-8, 10ab and 11, 12-13)

[*This Psalm describes Israel's King Solomon, but Christians apply its
imagery to Jesus who rules in justice and love.*]

Psalm 85

Response
**God is speaking peace,
peace to faithful people.**

Verses

I listen to God speaking:
God is speaking peace;
salvation is coming near,
glory is filling our land.

Love and fidelity embrace;
peace and justice kiss.
Fidelity sprouts from the earth;
justice leans down from heaven.

The Lord pours out riches;
our land springs to life.
Justice clears God's way
and peace keeps pace.
            (85:8ab and 9, 10-11, 12-13)

Psalm 91

Response
**My refuge, my fortress,
my God in whom I trust.**

Verses

All you sheltered by God Most High,
who live in the Almighty's shadow,
say to the Lord, "My refuge, my fortress,
my God in whom I trust!"

No evil shall ever touch you,
no harm come near your home.
God instructs angels
to guard you wherever you go.

With their hands they support you
so your foot will not strike a stone.
On lion and viper you shall tread,
trample tawny lion and dragon.

I will deliver all who cling to me,
raise the ones who know me.
These will I rescue and honor,
satisfy with long life,
and show my power to save.

(91:1-2, 10-11, 12-13, 14 and 15c-16)

Psalm 95

Response
**Come, bow down and worship;
listen today to God's voice.**

Verses

Come, sing with joy to God,
shout to our Savior, our Rock.
Enter God's presence with praise,
enter with shouting and song.

God the Lord is great,
over the gods like a king.
God cradles the depths of the earth,
holds fast the mountain peaks.
God shaped the ocean and owns it,
formed the earth by hand.

Come, bow down and worship,
kneel to the Lord our maker.
This is our God, our shepherd;
we are the flock led with care.

(95:1-2, 3-5, 6-7)

Psalm 98

Response
**The ends of the earth have seen
the victory of our God.**

Verses

Sing to the Lord a new song,
the Lord of wonderful deeds.
Right hand and holy arm
have brought victory to God.

God made that victory known,
revealed justice to nations,
remembered a merciful love
loyal to the house of Israel.

The ends of the earth have seen
the victory of our God.
Shout to the Lord, you earth,
break into song, into praise!

Sing praise to God with a harp,
with a harp and sound of music.
With sound of trumpet and horn,
shout to the Lord, our king.
   (98:1, 2-3b, 3c-4, 5-6)

Psalm 100

Response
**God is our shepherd,
and we the flock.**

Verses

Shout with joy, all earth, to the Lord,
serve the Lord with gladness,
enter God's presence with joy!

Know that the Lord is God,
our maker to whom we belong,
our shepherd, and we the flock.
Enter the temple gates,
the courtyard with thanks and praise;
give thanks and bless God's name.

Indeed the Lord is good,
"God is lasting love!"
faithful from age to age.

(100:1-2, 3, 4, 5)

Psalm 103

Response
**The Lord is tender and caring,
slow to anger, rich in love.**

Verses

My soul, bless the Lord:
all my being, bless God's name!
My soul, bless the Lord,
hold dear all God's gifts!

Bless God, who forgives your sin
and heals every illness,
who snatches you from death
and enfolds you with tender care,
who fills your life with richness
and gives you an eagle's strength.

The Lord is tender and caring,
slow to anger, rich in love.
God will not accuse us long,
nor hold our sins for trial,
nor exact from us in kind
what our sins deserve.

As high as heaven above earth,
so great God's love for believers.
as far as east from west,
so God removes our sins.
As tender as father to child,
so gentle is God to believers.

(103:1-2, 3-5, 8-10, 11-13)

Psalm 104

Response
**Lord, breathe your Spirit,
make the face of the earth come alive!**

Verses

I will bless you, God!
You fill the world with awe,
with a genius
that shapes every thing.

All look to you for food
when they hunger.
You give it lavishly, they feast;
You give it not, they fear.

No food, no breath,
they drop back into dust.
Breathe into them,
they rise from the dust;
the face of the earth is alive!

May God delight in creation,
love it for ever.
I will make God a song
for my whole life,
to give God joy,
who is a joy to me.

(104:1ab and 24cd, 27-29a, 29b-30, 31 and 33-4)

Psalm 118

Response
**This is the day the Lord made,
let us rejoice and be glad.**

Verses

Give thanks, the Lord is good,
"God is lasting love!"
Now let Israel say,
"God is lasting love!"

The Lord works with force,
right hand raised up high.
I shall not die but live
to tell the Lord's great deeds.

The stone the builders rejected
has become the cornerstone.
This is the work of the Lord,
how wonderful in our eyes.

$\qquad\qquad$ (118:1-2, 15c-17, 22-23)

Psalm 122

Response
**With joy I heard them say,
"We must go to God's house!"**

Verses

With joy I heard them say,
"We must go to God's house!"
And now, Jerusalem,
we stand inside your gates.

Jerusalem, the city so built
that city and temple are one.
To you the tribes must come,
every tribe of the Lord.

It is the law of Israel
to honor God's name.
The seats of law are here,
the thrones of David's line.

Pray peace for Jerusalem:
happiness for your homes,
safety inside your walls,
peace in your great houses.

For love of family with friends
I say, "Peace be with you!"
For love of God's own house
I pray for your good.

(122:1-2, 3-4b, 4c-5b, 6-7, 8-9)

Psalm 130

Response
**The Lord will bring mercy
and grant full pardon.**

Verses

From the depths I call to you,
Lord, hear my cry.
Catch the sound of my voice
raised up, pleading.

If you record our sins,
Lord, who survives?
But because you forgive
we stand in awe.

I trust in God's word,
I trust in the Lord.
More than sentries for dawn
I watch for the Lord.

More than sentries for dawn
let Israel watch.
The Lord will bring mercy,
grant full pardon.

The Lord will pardon Israel
All its sins.
(130:1-2, 3-4, 5-6b, 6c-8)

Psalm 136

Response
God is lasting love.

Verses

Our God is good, give thanks!
God is lasting love!
Our God of gods, give thanks!
God is lasting love!
Our Lord of lords, give thanks!
God is lasting love!

Alone the maker of worlds!
God is lasting love!
Made patterns for the sky!
God is lasting love!
Spread land on the sea!
God is lasting love!

Made bodies of great light!
God is lasting love!
The sun to rule the day!
God is lasting love!
The moon and stars, the night!
God is lasting love!

Kept us from defeat!
God is lasting love!
God feeds all living things!
God is lasting love!
God in heaven, be thanked!
God is lasting love!
(136:1-3, 4-6, 7-9, 24-26)

[Alternate response line: **God's love will last for ever!**]

Psalm 145

Response
**Let me sing the praise of God,
now and for ever.**

Verses

I will exalt you, God my king,
and for ever bless your name.
I will bless you every day,
and for ever praise your name.

Gracious and merciful is the Lord,
slow to anger, full of love.
The Lord is good in every way,
merciful to every creature.

Let your works praise you, Lord,
your faithful ones bless you.
Let them proclaim your glorious reign,
let them tell of your might.

The Lord is faithful in every word,
and gracious in every work.
The Lord supports the fallen,
raises those bowed down.
(145:1-2, 8-9, 10-11, 11c-14)

THE COMMON LECTIONARY

A promising trend in modern liturgical life is the growing use of a lectionary as the basis for the public reading of scripture. A lectionary is a listing of passages from the Bible which are arranged for systematic reading, especially in public worship.

The listing used in *Thankful Praise* is called the *Common Lectionary*. It is based on the lectionary developed by the Roman Catholic Church as part of its reform of worship following the second Vatican Council. Several protestant versions were developed, including one that Disciples have been using since the early 1970s. As the result of work done in 1976 by the United Methodist Church and the Consultation on Church Union, a consensus version was published and has been much used. The *Common Lectionary* takes this process one step further. The Consultation on Common Texts, an ecumenical group of worship scholars and executives, has reconciled the variations as much as is possible. They have also responded to some of the criticisms that the three-year lectionary has received since its first publication.

The three readings for each Sunday (one from the Hebrew Scriptures, one from an epistle, and one from a gospel) are selected because they coordinate with the drama of the Christian year. Thus, in Advent the readings focus on the coming of God, while in Easter they center on the meaning of the resurrection. In this way, the preacher and congregation are systematically exposed to the full range of texts and themes in the Christian tradition.

This table has been prepared for use in a wide range of Catholic and Protestant churches. Therefore, several of the special emphases will be unfamiliar to Disciples. Because some of these church traditions use readings from the Apocrypha, several selections from these books also appear in the table. Disciples following this table will need to make their own adaptations.

172

TABLE OF READINGS AND PSALMS

(Versification follows that of the Revised Standard Version)

	First Sunday of Advent	Second Sunday of Advent	Third Sunday of Advent	Fourth Sunday of Advent
A. Lesson 1	Isa 2:1-5 Ps 122	Isa 11:1-10 Ps 72:1-8	Isa 35:1-10 Ps 146:5-10	Isa 7:10-16 Ps 24
Lesson 2	Rom 13:11-14	Rom 15:4-13	James 5:7-10	Rom 1:1-7
Gospel	Matt 24:36-44	Matt 3:1-12	Matt 11:2-11	Matt 1:18-25
B. Lesson 1	Isa 63:16-64:8 Ps 80:1-7	Isa 40:1-11 Ps 85:8-13	Isa 61:1-4, 8-11 Luke 1:46b-55	2 Sam 7:8-16 Ps 89:1-4,19-24
Lesson 2	1 Cor 1:3-9	2 Peter 3:8-15a	1 Thess 5:16-24	Rom 16:25-27
Gospel	Mark 13:32-37	Mark 1:1-8	John 1:6-8, 19-28	Luke 1:26-38
C. Lesson 1	Jer 33:14-16 Ps 25:1-10	Baruch 5:1-9 or Mal 3:1-4 Ps 126	Zeph 3:14-20 Isa 12:2-6	Micah 5:2-5a (5:1-4a) Ps 80:1-7
Lesson 2	1 Thess 3:9-13	Phil 1:3-11	Phil 4:4-9	Heb 10:5-10
Gospel	Luke 21:25-36	Luke 3:1-6	Luke 3:7-18	Luke 1:39-55

	Christmas, First Proper (Christmas Eve/ Day)[1]	Christmas Second Proper (Add'l Lessons for Christmas Day)	Christmas Third Proper (Add'l Lessons for Christmas Day)
A. Lesson 1	Isa 9:2-7	Isa 62:6-7, 10-12	Isa 52:7-10
	Ps 96	Ps 97	Ps 98
Lesson 2	Titus 2:11-14	Titus 3:4-7	Hebr 1:1-12
Gospel	Luke 2:1-20	Luke 2:8-20	John 1:1-14

[1]The readings from the second and third propers for Christmas may be used as alternatives for Christmas day. If the third proper is not used on Christmas day, it should be used at some service during the Christmas cycle because of the significance of John's prologue.

	First Sunday after Christmas[2]	January 1- Name of Jesus Solemnity of Mary, Mother of God	January 1 (when observed as New Year)	Second Sunday after Christmas[3]
A. Lesson 1	Isa 63:7-9	Num 6:22-27	Deut 8:1-10	Jer 31:7-14 or Ecclus 24:1-4, 12-16
	Ps 111	Ps 67	Ps 117	Ps 147:12-20
Lesson 2	Heb 2:10-18	Gal 4:4-7 or Phil 2:9-13	Rev 21:1-6a	Eph 1:3-6, 15-18
Gospel	Matt 2:13-15, 19-23	Luke 2:15-21	Matt 25:31-46	John 1:1-18
B. Lesson 1	Isa 61:10-62:3 Ps 111		Eccles 3:1-13 Ps 8	
Lesson 2	Gal 4:4-7		Col 2:1-7	
Gospel	Luke 2:22-40		Matt 9:14-17	
C. Lesson 1	1 Sam 2:18-20, 26 or Ecclus 3:3-7, 14-17 Ps 111		Isa 49:1-10 Ps 90:1-12	
Lesson 2	Col 3:12-17		Eph 3:1-10	
Gospel	Luke 2:41-52		Luke 14:16-24	

[2]or the readings for Epiphany   [3]or the readings for Epiphany if not otherwise used.

175   *The Common Lectionary*

	Epiphany	Baptism of the Lord (1st Sun. after Epiphany)[4]	2nd Sunday after Epiphany	3rd Sunday after Epiphany	4th Sunday after Epiphany
A. Lesson 1	Isa 60:1-6 Ps 72:1-14	Isa 42:1-9 Ps 29	Isa 49:1-7 Ps 40:1-11	Isa 9:1-4 Ps 27:1-6	Micah 6:1-8 Ps 27:1-11
Lesson 2	Eph 3:1-12	Acts 10:34-43	1 Cor 1:1-9	1 Cor 1:10-17	1 Cor 1:18-31
Gospel	Matt 2:1-12	Matt 3:13-17	John 1:29-34	Matt 4:12-23	Matt 5:1-12
B. Lesson 1		Gen 1:1-5 Ps 29	1 Sam 3:1-10, (11-20) Ps 63:1-8	Jonah 3:1-5, 10 Ps 62:5-12	Deut 18:15-20 Ps 111
Lesson 2		Acts 19:1-7	1 Cor 6:12-20	1 Cor 7:29-31 (32-35)	1 Cor 8:1-13
Gospel		Mark 1:4-11	John 1:35-42	Mark 1:14-20	Mark 1:21-28
C. Lesson 1		Isa 61:1-4 Ps 29	Isa 62:1-5 Ps 36:5-10	Neh 8:1-4a, 5-6, 8-10 Ps 19:7-14	Jer 1:4-10 Ps 71:1-6
Lesson 2		Acts 8:14-17	1 Cor 12:1-11	1 Cor 12:12-30	1 Cor 13:1-13
Gospel		Luke 3:15-17, 21-22	John 2:1-11	Luke 4:14-21	Luke 4:21-30

[4]In Leap Years, the number of Sundays after Epiphany will be the same as if Easter Day were one day later.

	5th Sunday after Epiphany	6th Sunday after Epiphany (Proper 1)	7th Sunday after Epiphany (Proper 2)	8th Sunday after Epiphany (Proper 3)	Last Sunday after Epiphany Transfiguration
A. Lesson 1	Isa 58:3-9a	Deut 30:15-20 or Ecclus 15:15-20	Isa 49:8-13	Lev 19:1-2, 9-18	Exod 24:12-18
	Ps 112:4-9	Ps 119:1-8	Ps 62:5-12	Ps 119:33-40	Ps 2:6-11
Lesson 2	1 Cor 2:1-11	1 Cor 3:1-9	1 Cor 3:10-11, 16-23	1 Cor 4:1-5	2 Peter 1:16-21
Gospel	Matt 5:13-16	Matt 5:17-26	Matt 5:27-37	Matt 5:38-48	Matt 17:1-9
B. Lesson 1	Job 7:1-7 Ps 147:1-11	2 Kings 5:1-14 Ps 32	Isa 43:18-25 Ps 41	Hos 2:14-20 Ps 103:1-13	2 Kings 2:1-12a Ps 50:1-6
Lesson 2	1 Cor 9:16-23	1 Cor 9:24-27	2 Cor 1:18-22	2 Cor 3:1-6	2 Cor 4:3-6
Gospel	Mark 1:29-39	Mark 1:40-45	Mark 2:1-12	Mark 2:18-22	Mark 9:2-9
C. Lesson 1	Isa 6:1-8 (9-13) Ps 138	Jer 17:5-10 Ps 1	Gen 45:3-11, 15 Ps 37:1-11	Ecclus 27:4-7 or Isa 55:10-13 Ps 92:1-4, 12-15	Exod 34:29-35 Ps 99
Lesson 2	1 Cor 15:1-11	1 Cor 15:12-20	1 Cor 15:35-38, 42-50	1 Cor 15:51-58	2 Cor 3:12-4:2
Gospel	Luke 5:1-11	Luke 6:17-26	Luke 6:27-38	Luke 6:39-49	Luke 9:28-36

	Ash Wednesday	1st Sunday of Lent	2nd Sunday of Lent	3rd Sunday of Lent	4th Sunday of Lent
A. Lesson 1	Joel 2:1-2, 12-17a Ps 51:1-12	Gen 2:4b-9, 15-17, 25-3:7 Ps 130	Gen 12:1-4a (4b-8) Ps 33:18-22	Exod 17:3-7 Ps 95	1 Sam 16:1-3 Ps 23
Lesson 2	2 Cor 5:20b-6:2 (3-10)	Rom 5:12-19	Rom 4:1-5, (6-12), 13-17	Rom 5:1-11	Eph 5:8-14
Gospel	Matt 6:1-6, 16-21	Matt 4:1-11	John 3:1-17 or Matt 17:1-9	John 4:5-26 (27-42)	John 9:1-41
B. Lesson 1		Gen 9:8-17 Ps 25:1-10	Gen 17:1-10, 15-19 Ps 105:1-11	Exod 20:1-17 Ps 19:7-14	2 Chron 36:14-23 Ps 137:1-6
Lesson 2		1 Peter 3:18-22	Rom 4:16-25	1 Cor 1:22-25	Eph 2:4-10
Gospel		Mark 1:9-15	Mark 8:31-38 or Mark 9:1-9	John 2:13-22	John 3:14-21
C. Lesson 1		Deut 26:1-11 Ps 91:9-16	Gen 15:1-12, 17-18 Ps 127	Exod 3:1-15 Ps 103:1-13	Joshua 5:9-12 Ps 34:1-8
Lesson 2		Rom 10:8b-13	Phil 3:17-4:1	1 Cor 10:1-13	2 Cor 5:16-21
Gospel		Luke 4:1-13	Luke 13:31-35 or Luke 9:28-36	Luke 13:1-9	Luke 15:1-3, 11-32

	5th Sunday of Lent	Lent 6 when observed as Passion Sunday	Lent 6 observed as Palm Sunday[5]
A. Lesson 1	Ezek 37:1-14 Ps 116:1-9	Isa 50:4-9a Ps 31:9-16	Isa 50:4-9a Ps 118:19-29
Lesson 2	Rom 8:6-11	Phil 2:5-11	Phil 2:5-11
Gospel	John 11:(1-16), 17-45	Matt 26:14-27:66 or Matt 27:11-54	Matt 21:1-11
B. Lesson 1	Jer 31:31-34 Ps 51:10-17	Same as A Ps 31:9-16	Same as A Ps 118:19-29
Lesson 2	Heb 5:7-10	Same as A	Same as A
Gospel	John 12:20-33	Mark 14:1-15:47 or Mark 15:1-39	Mark 11:1-11 or John 12:12-16
C. Lesson 1	Isa 43:16-21 Ps 126	Same as A Ps 31:9-16	Same as A Ps 118:19-29
Lesson 2	Phil 3:8-14	Same as A	Same as A
Gospel	John 12:1-8	Luke 22:14-23:56 or Luke 23:1-49	Luke 19:28-40

[5]These readings are provided for the liturgy or procession of palms for churches which have not had the tradition of readings-and-procession and also for an early "said" service in the Episcopal tradition.

179 *The Common Lectionary*

Holy Week

	Monday	Tuesday	Wednesday	Holy Thursday[6] [7]	Good Friday
A. Lesson 1	Isa 42:1-9 Ps 36:5-10	Isa 49:1-7 Ps 71:1-12	Isa 50:4-9a Ps 70	Exod 12:1-4 Ps 116:12-19	Isa 52:13-53:12 Ps 22:1-18
Lesson 2	Heb 9:11-15	1 Cor 1:18-31	Heb 12:1-3	1 Cor 11:23-26	Heb 4:14-16, 5:7-9
Gospel	John 12:1-11	John 12:20-36	John 13:21-30	John 13:1-15	John 18:1-19:42 or John 19:17-30
B. Lesson 1				Exod 24:3-8 Ps 116:12-19	
Lesson 2				1 Cor 10:16-17	
Gospel				Mark 14:12-26	
C. Lesson 1				Jer 31:31-34 Ps 116:12-19	
Lesson 2				Heb 10:16-25	
Gospel				Luke 22:7-20	

[6]for those who want the feet washing every year, "A" readings are used each year.
[7]Psalm 116 is used at the Lord's Supper on Holy Thursday. Psalm 89:20-21, 24, 26 is used at the "chrism" service.

180   *The Common Lectionary*

Easter Vigil[8]

Old Testament Readings and Psalms (A, B, C)

Genesis 1:1-2:2
    Psalm 33
Genesis 7:1-5, 11-18; 8:6-18; 9:8-13
    Psalm 46
Genesis 22:1-18
    Psalm 16
Exodus 14:10-15:1
Exodus 15:1-6, 11-13, 17-18
Isaiah 54:5-14
    Psalm 30
Isaiah 55:1-11
Isaiah 12:2-6
Baruch 3:9-15, 32-4:4
    Psalm 19

Ezekiel 36:24-28
    Psalm 42
Ezekiel 37:1-14
    Psalm 143
Zephaniah 3:14-20
    Psalm 98

Second Reading (A, B, C)
Romans 6:3-11
    Psalm 114

Gospel
  A. Matthew 28:1-10
  B. Mark 16:1-8
  C. Luke 24:1-12

[8]This selection of readings and psalms is provided for the Easter Vigil. A minimum of three readings from the Old Testament should be used, and this should always include Exodus 14.

181. *The Common Lectionary*

	Easter[9]	2nd Sunday of Easter	3rd Sunday of Easter	4th Sunday of Easter	5th Sunday of Easter
A. Lesson 1	Acts 10:34-43 or Jer 31:1-6 Ps 118:14-24	Acts 2:14a, 22-32 Ps 16:5-11	Acts 2:14a, 36-41 Ps 116:12-19	Acts 2:42-47 Ps 23	Acts 7:55-60 Ps 31:1-8
Lesson 2	Col 3:1-4 or Acts 10:34-43	1 Peter 1:3-9	1 Peter 1:17-23	1 Peter 2:19-25	1 Peter 2:2-10
Gospel	John 20:1-18 or Matt 28:1-10	John 20:19-31	Luke 24:13-35	John 10:1-10	John 14:1-14
B. Lesson 1	Acts 10:34-43 or Isa 25:6-9 Ps 118:14-24	Acts 4:32-35 Ps 133	Acts 3:12-19 Ps 4	Acts 4:8-12 Ps 23	Acts 8:26-40 Ps 22:25-31
Lesson 2	1 Cor 15:1-11 or Acts 10:34-43	1 John 1:1-2:2	1 John 3:1-7	1 John 3:18-24	1 John 4:7-12
Gospel	John 20:1-18 or Mark 16:1-8	John 20:19-31	Luke 24:35-48	John 10:11-18	John 15:1-8

C. Lesson 1	Acts 10:34-43 or Isa 65:17-25 Ps 118:14-24	Acts 5:27-32 Ps 2	Acts 9:1-20 Ps 30:4-12	Acts 13:15-16, 26-33 Ps 23	Acts 14:8-18 Ps 145:3b-21
Lesson 2	1 Cor 15:19-26 or Acts 10:34-43	Rev 1:4-8	Rev 5:11-14	Rev 7:9-17	Rev 21:1-6
Gospel	John 20:1-18 or Luke 24:1-12	John 20:19-31	John 21:1-19 or John 21:15-19	John 10:22-30	John 13:31-35

[9]If the Old Testament passage is chosen, the Acts passage is used as the second reading to initiate the sequential reading of Acts during the fifty days of Easter.

Easter Evening[10]

A. Lesson 1	Acts 5:29-32 or Dan 12:1-3 Ps 150
Lesson 2	1 Cor 5:6-8 or Acts 5:29-32
Gospel	Luke 24:13-49

[10]If the first reading is from the Old Testament, the reading from Acts should be second.

	6th Sunday of Easter	Ascension[11]	7th Sunday of Easter	Pentecost[12]	Trinity Sunday
A. Lesson 1	Acts 17:22-31 Ps 66:8-20	Acts 1:1-11 Ps 47	Acts 1:6-14 Ps 68:1-10	Acts 2:1-21 or Isa 44:1-8 Ps 104:24-34	Deut 4:32-40 Ps 33:1-12
Lesson 2	1 Peter 3:13-22	Eph 1:15-23	1 Peter 4:12-14; 5:6-11	1 Cor 12:3b-13 or Acts 2:1-21	2 Cor 13:5-14
Gospel	John 14:15-21	Luke 24:46-53 or Mark 16:9-16, 19-20	John 17:1-11	John 20:19-23 or John 7:37-39	Matt 28:16-20
B. Lesson 1	Acts 10:44-48 Ps 98	Ps 47	Acts 1:15-17, 21-26 Ps 1	Acts 2:1-21 or Ezek 37:1-14 Ps 104:24-34	Isa 6:1-8 Ps 29
Lesson 2	1 John 5:1-6		1 John 5:9-13	Rom 8:22-27 or Acts 2:1-21	Rom 8:12-17
Gospel	John 15:9-17		John 17:11b-19	John 15:26-27; 16:4b-15	John 3:1-17
C. Lesson 1	Acts 15:1-2, 22-29 Ps 67	Ps 47	Acts 16:16-34 Ps 97	Acts 2:1-21 or Gen 11:1-9 Ps 104:24-34	Prov 8:22-31 Ps 8
Lesson 2	Rev 21:10, 22-27		Rev 22:12-14, 16-17, 20	Rom 8:14-17 or Acts 2:1-21	Rom 5:1-5
Gospel	John 14:23-29		John 17:20-26	John 14:8-17,	John 16:12-15, 25-27

[11]Or on the Seventh Sunday of Easter.
[12]If the Old Testament passage is chosen for the first reading, the Acts passage is used as the second reading.

	Proper 4[13] Sunday between May 29 and June 4 inclusive (if after Trinity Sunday)	Proper 5 Sunday between June 5 and 11 inclusive (if after Trinity Sunday)	Proper 6 Sunday between June 12 and 18 inclusive (if after Trinity Sunday)	Proper 7 Sunday between June 19 and 25 inclusive (if after Trinity Sunday)	Proper 8 Sunday between June 26 and July 2 inclusive
A. Lesson 1	Gen 12:1-9 Ps 33:12-22	Gen 22:1-18 Ps 13	Gen 25:19-34 Ps 46	Gen 28:10-17 Ps 91:1-10	Gen 32:22-32 Ps 17:1-7, 15
Lesson 2	Rom 3:21-28	Rom 4:13-18	Rom 5:6-11	Rom 5:12-19	Rom 6:3-11
Gospel	Matt 7:21-29	Matt 9:9-13	Matt 9:35-10:8	Matt 10:24-33	Matt 10:34-42
B. Lesson 1	1 Sam 16:1-13 Ps 20	1 Sam 16:14-23 Ps 57	2 Sam 1:1, 17-27 Ps 46	2 Sam 5:1-12 Ps 48	2 Sam 6:1-15 Ps 24
Lesson 2	2 Cor 4:5-12	2 Cor 4:13-5:1	2 Cor 5:6-10, 14-17	2 Cor 5:18-6:2	2 Cor 8:7-15
Gospel	Mark 2:23-3:6	Mark 3:20-35	Mark 4:26-34	Mark 4:35-41	Mark 5:21-43
C. Lesson 1	1 Kgs 8:22-23, 41-43 Ps 100	1 Kgs 17:17-24 Ps 113	1 Kgs 19:1-8 Ps 42	1 Kgs 19:9-14 Ps 43	1 Kgs 19:15-21 Ps 44:1-8
Lesson 2	Gal 1:1-10	Gal 1:11-24	Gal 2:15-21	Gal 3:23-39	Gal 5:1,13-25
Gospel	Luke 7:1-10	Luke 7:11-17	Luke 7:36-8:3	Luke 9:18-24	Luke 9:51-62

[13]If the Sunday between May 24 and 28 inclusive follows Trinity Sunday, use Eighth Sunday after Epiphany on that day.

185 *The Common Lectionary*

		Proper 9 Sunday between July 3 and 9 inclusive	Proper 10 Sunday between July 10 and 16 inclusive	Proper 11 Sunday between July 17 and 23 inclusive	Proper 12 Sunday between July 24 and 30 inclusive	Proper 13 Sunday between July 31 and Aug. 6 inclusive
A.	Lesson 1	Exod 1:6-14, 22-2:10 Ps 124	Exod 2:11-22 Ps 69:6-15	Exod 3:1-12 Ps 103:1-13	Exod 3:13-20 Ps 105:1-11	Exod 12:1-14 Ps 143:1-10
	Lesson 2	Rom 7:14-25a	Rom 8:9-17	Rom 8:18-25	Rom 8:26-30	Rom 8:31-39
	Gospel	Matt 11:25-30	Matt 13:1-9, 18-23	Matt 13:24-30, 36-43	Matt 13:44-52	Matt 14:13-21
B.	Lesson 1	2 Sam 7:1-17 Ps 89:20-37	2 Sam 7:18-29 Ps 132:11-18	2 Sam 11:1-15 Ps 53	2 Sam 12:1-14 Ps 32	2 Sam 12:15b-24 Ps 34:11-22
	Lesson 2	2 Cor 12:1-10	Eph 1:1-10	Eph 2:11-22	Eph 3:14-21	Eph 4:1-6
	Gospel	Mark 6:1-6	Mark 6:7-13	Mark 6:30-34	John 6:1-15	John 6:24-35
C.	Lesson 1	1 Kgs 21:1-3, 17-21 Ps 5:1-8	2 Kgs 2:1,6-14 Ps 139:1-12	2 Kgs 4:8-17 Ps 139:13-18	2 Kgs 5:1-15ab ("...in Israel") Ps 21:1-7	2 Kgs 13:14-20a Ps 28
	Lesson 2	Gal 6:7-18	Col 1:1-14	Col 1:21-29	Col 2:6-15	Col 3:1-11
	Gospel	Luke 10:1-12, 17-20	Luke 10:25-37	Luke 10:38-42	Luke 11:1-13	Luke 12:13-21

	Proper 14 Sunday between Aug 7 and 13 inclusive	Proper 15 Sunday between Aug 14 and 20 inclusive	Proper 16 Sunday between Aug 21 and 27 inclusive	Proper 17 Sunday between Aug 28 and Sep 3 inclusive	Proper 18 Sunday between Sep 4 and 10 inclusive
A. Lesson 1	Exod 14:19-31 Ps 106:4-12	Exod 16:2-15 Ps 78:1-3, 10-20	Exod 17:1-7 Ps 95	Exod 19:1-9 Ps 114	Exod 19:16-24 Ps 115:1-11
Lesson 2	Rom 9:1-5	Rom 11:13-16, 29-32	Rom 11:33-36	Rom 12:1-13	Rom 13:1-10
Gospel	Matt 14:22-33	Matt 15:21-28	Matt 16:13-20	Matt 16:21-28	Matt 18:15-20
B. Lesson 1	1 Sam 18:1, 5, 9-15 Ps 143:1-8	2 Sam 18:24-33 Ps 102:1-12	2 Sam 23:1-7 Ps 67	1 Kgs 2:1-4, 10-12 Ps 121	Ecclus 5:8-15 or Prov 2:1-8 Ps 119:129-136
Lesson 2	Eph 4:25-5:2	Eph 5:15-20	Eph 5:21-33	Eph 6:10-20	James 1:17-27
Gospel	John 6:35, 41-51	John 6:51-58	John 6:55-69	Mark 7:1-8, 14-15, 21-23	Mark 7:31-37
C. Lesson 1	Jer 18:1-11 Ps 14	Jer 20:7-13 Ps 10:12-18	Jer 28:1-9 Ps 84	Ezek 18:1-9, 25-29 Ps 15	Ezek 33:1-11 Ps 94:12-22
Lesson 2	Heb 11:1-3, 8-19	Heb 12:1-2, 12-17	Heb 12:18-29	Heb 13:1-8	Philemon 1-20
Gospel	Luke 12:32-40	Luke 12:49-56	Luke 13:22-30	Luke 14:1, 7-14	Luke 14:25-33

187 *The Common Lectionary*

	Proper 19 Sunday between Sep 11 and 17 inclusive	Proper 20 Sunday between Sep 18 and 24 inclusive	Proper 21 Sunday between Sep 25 and Oct 1 inclusive	Proper 22 Sunday between Oct 2 and 8 inclusive	Proper 23 Sunday between Oct 9 and 15 inclusive
A. Lesson 1	Exod 20:1-20 Ps 19:7-14	Exod 32:1-14 Ps 106:7-8, 19-23	Exod 33:12-23 Ps 99	Num 27:12-23 Ps 81:1-10	Deut 34:1-12 Ps 135:1-14
Lesson 2	Rom 14:5-12	Phil 1:21-27	Phil 2:1-13	Phil 3:12-21	Phil 4:1-9
Gospel	Matt 18:21-35	Matt 20:1-16	Matt 21:28-32	Matt 21:33-43	Matt 22:1-14
B. Lesson 1	Prov 22:1-2, 8-9 Ps 125	Job 28:20-28 Ps 27:1-6	Job 42:1-6 Ps 27:7-14	Gen 2:18-24 Ps 128	Gen 3:8-19 Ps 90:1-12
Lesson 2	James 2:1-5, 8-10, 14-17	James 3:13-18	James 4:13-17, 5:7-11	Heb 1:1-4, 2:9-11	Heb 4:1-3, 9-13
Gospel	Mark 8:27-38	Mark 9:30-37	Mark 9:38-50	Mark 10:2-16	Mark 10:17-30
C. Lesson 1	Hos 4:1-3, 5:15-6:6 Ps 77:11-20	Hos 11:1-11 Ps 107:1-9	Joel 2:23-30 Ps 107:1, 33-43	Amos 5:6-7, 10-15 Ps 101	Micah 1:2;2:1-10 Ps 26
Lesson 2	1 Tim 1:12-17	1 Tim 2:1-7	1 Tim 6:6-19	2 Tim 1:1-14	2 Tim 2:8-15
Gospel	Luke 15:1-10	Luke 16:1-13	Luke 16:19-31	Luke 17:5-10	Luke 17:11-19

	Proper 24 Sunday between Oct 16 and 22 inclusive	Proper 25 Sunday between Oct 23 and 29 inclusive	Proper 26 Sunday between Oct 30 and Nov 5 inclusive	Proper 27 Sunday between Nov 6 and 12 inclusive	Proper 28 Sunday between Nov 13 and 19 inclusive
A. Lesson 1	Ruth 1:1-19a Ps 146	Ruth 2:1-13 Ps 128	Ruth 4:7-17 Ps 127	Amos 5:18-14 Ps 50:7-15	Zeph 1:7, 12-18 Ps 76
Lesson 2	1 Thess 1:1-10	1 Thess 2:1-8	1 Thess 2:9-13, 17-20	1 Thess 4:13-18	1 Thess 5:1-11
Gospel	Matt 22:15-22	Matt 22:34-46	Matt 23:1-12	Matt 25:1-13	Matt 25:14-30
B. Lesson 1	Isa 53:7-12 Ps 35:17-28	Jer 31:7-9 Ps 126	Deut 6:1-9 Ps 119:33-48	1 Kgs 17:8-16 Ps 146	Dan 7:9-14 Ps 145:8-13
Lesson 2	Heb 4:14-16	Heb 5:1-6	Heb 7:23-28	Heb 9:24-28	Heb 10:11-18
Gospel	Mark 10:35-45	Mark 10:46-52	Mark 12:28-34	Mark 12:38-44	Mark 13:24-32
C. Lesson 1	Hab 1:1-3, 2:1-4 Ps 119:137-144	Zeph 3:1-9 Ps 3	Hag 2:1-9 Ps 65:1-8	Zech 7:1-10 Ps 9:11-20	Mal 4:1-6 (3:19-24 in Heb.) Ps 82
Lesson 2	2 Tim 3:14-4:5	2 Tim 4:6-8, 16-18	2 Thess 1:5-12	2 Thess 2:13-3:5	2 Thess 3:6-13
Gospel	Luke 18:1-8	Luke 18:9-14	Luke 19:1-10	Luke 20:27-38	Luke 21:5-19

189   *The Common Lectionary*

Proper 29
(Christ the King)
Sunday between
Nov 20 and 26
inclusive

A. Lesson 1	Ezek 34:11-16, 20-24	
	Ps 23	
Lesson 2	1 Cor 15:20-28	
Gospel	Matt 25:31-46	
B. Lesson 1	Jer 23:1-6	
	Ps 93	
Lesson 2	Rev 1:4b-8	
Gospel	John 18:33-37	
C. Lesson 1	2 Sam 5:1-5	
	Ps 95	
Lesson 2	Col 1:11-20	
Gospel	John 12:9-19	

	Annunciation March 25	Visitation May 31	Presentation February 2	Holy Cross September 14
A. Lesson 1	Isa 7:10-14 Ps 45 or 40:6-10	1 Sam 2:1-10 Ps 113	Mal 3:1-4 Ps 84 or 24:7-10	Num 21:4b-9 Ps 98:1-5 or 78:1-2,34-38
Lesson 2	Heb 10:4-10	Rom 12:9-16b	Heb 2:14-18	1 Cor 1:18-24
Gospel	Luke 1:26-38	Luke 1:39-57	Luke 2:22-40	John 3:13-17

	All Saints, November 1[14]	Thanksgiving Day[15]
A. Lesson 1	Rev 7:9-17 Ps 34:1-10	Deut 8:7-18 Ps 65
Lesson 2	1 John 3:1-3	2 Cor 9:6-15
Gospel	Matt 5:1-12	Luke 17:11-19
B. Lesson 1	Rev 21:1-6a Ps 24:1-6	Joel 2:21-27 Ps 126
Lesson 2	Col 1:9-14	1 Tim 2:1-7
Gospel	John 11:32-44	Matt 6:25-33
C. Lesson 1	Dan 7:1-3, 15-18 Ps 149	Deut 26:1-11 Ps 100
Lesson 2	Eph 1:11-23	Phil 4:4-9
Gospel	Luke 6:20-36	John 6:25-35

[14]or on first day in November.
[15]readings *ad libitum*, not tied to A, B, or C.

ACKNOWLEDGMENTS

The following publishers and authors are gratefully acknowledged:

The International Consultation on English Texts and Fortress Press for permission to reprint translations of ecumenical liturgical texts, including the Lord's Prayer, the Apostles Creed, and the Nicene Creed, from *Prayers We Have in Common*, Second Revised Edition, 1975.

The International Commission on English in the Liturgy for permission to use portions of twenty-two Psalms published as part of its Psalter Project.

The Consultation on Common Texts for permission to reprint the list of readings from *The Common Lectionary: The Lectionary Proposed by the Consultation on Common Texts. Copyright, 1983.*

Numbers 16, 17 from *The Communion Service: A Model for Christian Churches (Disciples of Christ)*, by Keith Watkins; 38 Jennifer Riggs (alt.); 93-97 adapted from *On A Friday Afternoon*, by Hans-Reudi Weber (Eerdmans, 1979), 99 adapted from *Way of the Cross, Way of Justice*, by Leonardo Boff (Orbis, 1980); 158, 159 John R. Johnson (alt.); 161 *God's Trombones*, by James Weldon Johnson, Viking, 1927, used by permission; 162 *Book of Common Prayer*; 176 *Christian Worship: A Service Book*, by G. Edwin Osborn, CBP Press, 1953; 181 *Alone with God*, by J. H. Garrison, 1891; 189 *Jesus Christ: The Life of the World*, p. 102; 190 *An Order of Worship*, Consultation on Church Union, 1968, pp. 28-33; 191 *Ecumenical Perspectives on Baptism, Eucharist and Ministry*, ed. by Max Thurian, World Council of Churches, 1983, pp. 241-246); 192 *Confessing Our Faith Around the World*, ed. by Hans-Georg Link, World Council of Churches, 1984, vol. III, pp. 47-51.